ADDICTIONARY

The Resource Lexicon

For Counselors, Addicts, Alcoholics,
and Affected Families and Friends

ADDICTIONARY

The Resource Lexicon

For Counselors, Addicts, Alcoholics,
and Affected Families and Friends

©Richard K. Horton, MSEd, LADC

A Three Owls Production

2017

ADDICTIONARY

The Resource Lexicon

For Counselors, Addicts, Alcoholics,
and Affected Families and Friends

Copyright © 2017 by the author

ISBN 978-1536877168

Available from

www.createspace.com/6462609

www.amazon.com

and directly from the Publisher:

Richard K. Horton
20 Feyler's Corner
Waldoboro, ME 04572

ACKNOWLDEGMENTS

I know that in listing some I will have forgotten many during my work as a substance abuse counselor in the Maine State Prison system. I honor and value: Mikey B., Mikey C., Dave R., Chris C., Henry L., Peter L., Brandon L., Andre H. (father and son), Scott A., Randy H., Dickie and Jimmy E., Shawn D., Jake S., Matt D., Lance P., Greg W., Sam T., Sam B., Kai N., Zack K., Tim and Tom W., Larry B. Last initials indicate former (or current) inmates and clients. Don't make me come over there! Colleagues include Paul Quijano, Stu Zubrod, Diane White, Leida Dardis, Gerry LaChapelle, Rick Ivey, Tom Roach, Al Barlow, Mae Worcester, Sue Dumond, Big Ray Felt, and so many more. If I've left you out, please understand that I knew over 2300 men as clients over my sixteen years with the DOC. There are many faces I remember, though the names may have left me, and I'm grateful to you all. It's not possible to be a good counselor without the willingness to learn from one's clients.

To Bill Tanner and Jeff Bickford and those who worked with them, I thank you for my introduction to correctional work, where I first learned that inmates are human beings. Also to Henry G., the first inmate I ever laid eyes on right after his arrest for a crime that imprisons him still. He looked fierce and mean when I regarded him through the pod door, and he glared at me, and I thought, "What the hell have I gotten myself into?" Over 20 years later I got to know him for the decent human being he is, and he allowed me to travel full circle.

To Margaret Kimble, for insight, support, compassion, wisdom, and, finally, friendship.

Strong appreciation goes to my new friend, Judy Knowlton, for turning me on to createspace.com, and for the rapidity with which she became a new friend I've known all my life.

A special *non*-dedication to Mike T., for embodying the definition of the word *punk* (which is not defined in this volume). *See* **Resentment.**

A special shout out to my son, Nick, for his heroic self-work, and to his wife, Jen, for hers. Also to my daughters, Ashley and Edan. And to my grandson, Calai, who said, with great wisdom (*See* **Abuse**) when I asked if I could eat his arm, replied, *"No! I am not for eating."*

To people who have impacted strongly in my life and helped me become the adult I have become: Andre Taylor, Al Sloane, Nol Putnam, David Southworth (RIP), John Risley, Andy Makoto Tanaka.

And to my parents, who taught me more than they knew.

About the Author

Richard K. Horton has been a substance abuse counselor for roughly twenty years. Beginning his career as a teacher, he quickly found counseling more his forte and went to graduate school for his Masters in Counseling. Before too long he became a facilitator for the Navy Alcohol and Drug Safety Action Program. His next position was with Community Correctional Services in Maine, a program with counselors serving jail populations in seven counties. This led to sixteen years of work within the Maine State Prison system, where he developed and adapted several group programs which would ultimately serve over 2300 men before a change in employer led to a program which, while effective, served fewer inmates in a more-restrictive sentence bracket.

The author is the originator of *Con Game*™, a unique therapeutic game whose original *Correctional Edition* was used with great success for sixteen years in substance abuse groups in the Maine State Prison System. It was also used in the training of employees new to the system. Its success led to the development of several other editions: *Men's Group* (also used in the prison), *Women's Group, High School, College, Family, Rehab, and Juvenile Drug Court,* with an *LGBT Edition* in the works. For information about this incisive, challenging, and rewarding game, please contact the author at the above email address.

Rick is also the author of a manual-based program, *Return to Self©*, now also available in Power Point format. This is a twelve-session group program appropriate not only for addicts and alcoholics, but also for anyone interested in working on life exploration and change.

For questions, comments, suggestions, or any other reasons, the author can be contacted at congame@roadrunner.com.

~ Dedication ~

This work is dedicated to those who fight their addictions and other demons, whether they win or lose. These are the unsung heroes of this world:

To the many clients who have taught me and accepted me as one who can try to help. I thank you from the bottom of my heart for allowing me to witness your miracles:

To the colleagues with whom I have worked, those who have accepted and nurtured my often unusual style and methods:

And to my wife, Judith Mitchell, who has supported me not only through our twenty years of marriage, but also, in absentia, for the years we were apart after she was my art teacher for my first two years of high school. You allowed a frightened, insecure young boy to experience a sense of worth when such experience was very hard for him to find. You continue to do so. You are my love, my best friend, my champion.

~ Note ~

This volume – indeed, much of my life – would not be possible were it not for Pia and Pat Mellody and all the counselors at The Meadows in Arizona and to the Peers present while I was there. Thank you for everything.

~ Foreword ~

Back in the ancient days following the 60's, when drug rehab programs were springing up like zits on adolescents I was working with LA street kids trying to get them past drug use in their lives. I was surprised to discover that they invented their own dynamic language to express their alienation, belonging and that these descriptive terms were an intimate part of their nascent ability to gradually separate from the drug culture. Each aspect of their experience had to be named so their perspective outside the problem could strengthen. As example: In listening to the endless litany of excuses why their problems were always someone else's hang-up, my intuition drop kicked a term into my head to describe this invisible and unreal "them." The term was "scapeghost." The term itself brought the dynamics of blame, projections, disowning responsibility, scapegoating and being scapegoated, and the idea of being haunted by death (change) into dialogue, a synthesis not easily rendered abstract, i.e. "just words." Addicts are wounded people, not malformed machines. In using creative terms less conceptual the emotions necessary to healing are embodied. They have impact and connection that the rationalizing ego can't quickly avoid. Psyche, in her endless creativity, put me onto this displacement of responsibility with a fresh term that immediately caught on and became part of the program's push to help the clients recognize, relate and eventually change this pattern that was such a key mechanism of drug abuse thinking.

This book, *Addictionary*, is a good, solid compilation of ideas, terms, phrases and stories that show the creative response to addictions that can easily seem "fixed in their brokenness." It is written by an author with extensive experience and insight in this work. He shares not only what has proven to be effective but also the spirit of this creative and authentic approach. Whether you have a wordsmith in your staff, clients, or not- YOU NEED THIS BOOK!

Lucas Sylvester

[After college and a few degrees L. Sylvester became a dedicated pupil of Jungian Psychology. He has taught and worked in the field since '72 in varied positions ranging from line staff, case management, to clinical director. His professional interests encompass dream/symptom analysis, spirituality, creativity, the schizophrenias, personality disorders and trauma. He is currently semi-retired with a talented wife/painter, writing about the symbolism of magic and continuing a small private practice in Midcoast Maine. He spends the season out on his boat, the Island Fox, at the helm on the flying bridge exploring the beauty and wonder of nature and the moment beyond words.]

Lucas has an MA in Psychology and BA s in Philosophy and Psychology

Authors Note:

Everything in this volume is true. Note that I didn't say "factual," for there is a major difference between the two terms. Facts are facts, cold, hard, and certain. Truth, on the other hand, is colored by opinion, faith, one's baggage, and many other influences. For example, suppose I say to a friend, "My wife is more beautiful than yours." While that may be true to me, his truth might be completely at odds with mine. I will stand behind everything in this booklet and accept that others may see things very differently. After all, in the paths of recovery, there are no certainties.

Those who have been my clients will find that this volume is written almost precisely the way I speak when I counsel. It is informal, and it is written with the compassion and love with which I do my work. Please accept it in that way.

When the wolf is at the door,

    it's okay to use the window.

RK Horton

~ ~ ~ ~ ~ ~ ~ ~ ~ ~ ~ ~

Things may look bleak at

    the moment of occurrence,

But at least we ain't got locusts.

Jack Soo (Agent Yemana, from *Barney Miller*)

ADDICTIONARY

For Addicts, Alcoholics, and Their Friends and Families

Compiled, often with tongue in cheek,

but also with serious intent,

by

©Richard K. Horton, MSEd, LADC

The contents of this volume are in alphabetical order except for the Appendices

ADDICTIONARY..	**Pages 1 - 54**
APPENDIX 1 – Effects of Alcohol at Different BAC Levels....................................	Page A
APPENDIX 2 – BAC Levels – How much can you drink without being over the limit?.........	Page D
APPENDIX 3 - Categories & types of drugs, and their effects..................................	Page G
APPENDIX 4 – The Effects of Violence on Children..	Page K
APPENDIX 5 – The Addicted Family..	Page M
APPENDIX 6 – The Twelve Steps of Alcoholics Anonymous..................................	Page O
APPENDIX 7 – KARPMAN'S TRIANGLE OR DRAMA SYSTEM..........................	Page Q
APPENDIX 8 – Drugs Used in Opioid Addiction Treatment....................................	Page R
APPENDIX 9 – Johari's Window..	Page W
APPENDIX 10 – Myths and Addendums (in other words, items I forgot)..............	Page BB
APPENDIX 11 – Drug Terms..	Page FF

Addictionary:

For Addicts, Alcoholics, and Their Friends and Families

Come on, who's going to sit down and read a *dictionary?* Borrrrrrring!

A dictionary gives us nice, precise definitions of words. *Addictionary* gives us practical definitions that can be easily understood in the context of addiction and recovery. While a dictionary might define blame, for example, as *the responsibility for anything deserving of censure*, this volume defines it as *a defense mechanism that allows us to go through life without owning responsibility for anything we do or have done,* or *holding others responsible for everything that happens to us.* The dictionary definition is not wrong, certainly, but in terms of recovery and addiction, it means something a little different.

Addictionary, then, is a user-friendly guide to relevant terms for the recovery layman. While it may not exactly match the aforementioned volumes, it *is* accurate and can help addicts and those connected to them to gain some understanding of addiction and recovery from a non-technical point of view. All definitions in this book are related to recovery and addiction and are not to be confused with those "normal" definitions, whatever normal may be. These terms come from my extensive experience with addiction, dysfunction, and counseling.

In other words, the purpose of *Addictionary* is to tell people what the terms *mean* in real life. It is designed to offer a better understanding of addiction and recovery for the people connected to addicts as well as to people with other forms of dysfunction (believe me, they are innumerable). Is it complete? Doubtful, but it's a start.

It is important for the addicted users, as well as their affected others, to realize that there are many different models of treating addiction, with none being seen as absolutely the right way (except, perhaps, by their practitioners. After all, we use that in which we believe). Some methods work better for some people; for example, while it's a highly successful program, AA does not work for every alcoholic – and even when it does work, its success rate is roughly 20% (this increases when it is combined with therapy) (*See* **Alcoholics Anonymous**) .

The Downward Spiral

The following diagram, **Breaking the Cycle of Stinkin' Thinkin'**, refers to the *downward spiral* so often mentioned by those connected with the recovery process. While it is fairly self-explanatory, it may still bear some discussion.

Addicts are often given *external* clues that they might benefit by changing their behaviors. These include legal problems, accidents, injuries, and the comments of their families, their friends, and perhaps strangers (including innocent bystanders, clergy, law-enforcement individuals, etc.).

The external clues lead to *internal* clues, which, of course, are feelings: Joy, Pain, Fear, Loneliness, Anger, Guilt, and Shame (see **Emotions**). Addicts are unfamiliar with these emotions, having built up years of avoidance or stuffing by using their addictions.

When the internal clues – the feelings the addicts cannot handle – rear their ugly heads, they turn once again to the drug, behavior, or person of choice, which, of course, leads to the collection of more external clues, and the cycle is born and thus continues.

Looks pretty hopeless, doesn't it? Take heart, be of good cheer, and stay tuned for the second diagram.

Breaking the Cycle of Stinkin' Thinkin'
How do you figure out if there is a problem?

Do I have a problem? How did I end up here? What, if anything, is wrong with what I'm doing?

Inappropriate Coping Mechanisms

Drinking, drugging, behaviors such as raging, criminal activities, etc., used to numb, escape, or hide from the internal clues...

We receive

External Clues

OUI's, accidents, comments from family and friends, losses (family, friends, jobs, possessions, houses), legal problems, jail/prison time...

which lead to more

which lead to

which lead to

Internal Clues

Remorse, pain, fear, loneliness, anger, guilt, shame, conscience...

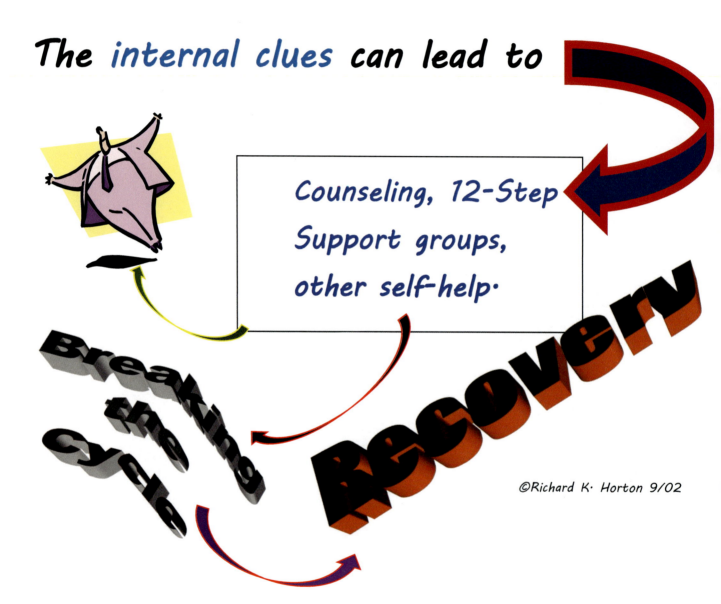

The only place in which change can occur is in the Internal Clues phase. Addicts may be able to stop using for a while due to jail, probation, or the pressure of friends and loved ones, but true change can occur only when they realize that the internal clues, the *feelings*, are not only a necessary part of life, but also ones which can actually be handled without the addiction.

I hope this makes the Downward Spiral easier to picture and understand. People have used the term probably since the invention of recovery. I believe that sometimes it helps to, as they say, "draw you a diagram." Now you've got one.

- A -

AA: *see* **Alcoholics Anonymous.**

Abandonment: *rejection, usually as a child, by a caregiver. Can result in feelings of insecurity, self-blame, worthlessness, shame. Can be felt by any child neglected by one or both parents; very common among adopted children despite the love of adoptive parents.*

Science has shown that newborns can recognize their mothers. It stands to reason, therefore, that they can also recognize their father if he has been present during the pregnancy and he has spoken. On some level, therefore, newborns and older children can recognize the *absence* of a parent, on some level they are unable to articulate, and thus experience their first loss and rejection.

Abuse: *the misuse of a living being by someone with more power. The destruction of safety. Falls under several categories, the lines between which are often somewhat blurry.*

Substance abuse: the use of a substance for other than its prescribed purpose.

Child abuse: oddly enough, the use of a child for other than its prescribed purpose.

There are five kinds of abuse.

- *Physical*: including hitting, kicking, pinching, squeezing, pulling hair/ears/arms – in short, any overt contact against the child's wishes that is not directly related to the positive care of the child (such as pulling out of danger, bathing, etc.).
- *Psychological/Emotional*: constantly belittling, shaming and humiliating a child; calling the child names to minimize his self-worth; threatening a child; isolating a child from other relatives or friends; constantly ignoring a child; encouraging a child to act inappropriately.
- *Intellectual*: disrespect for child's learning style, way of thinking or intellectual interests; ridiculing a child's carefully thought out ideas or devaluing a person's opinions; calling a child 'stupid' or 'slow.'
- *Sexual*: inappropriate touching; sexualizing activities; inappropriate sharing (parent's date, pornography, etc.); incest; any behavior not directly related to the positive care of the child (infants & toddlers – washing, etc.).

  {NOTE – Sexual abuse, contrary to the beliefs of many, may not automatically be considered *physical* abuse. While always inappropriate, it may actually feel physically good to the victim (we are not speaking of infant or child rape), which explains why a) males abused by older

- females tend to actually be proud of themselves), b) victims often blame themselves not necessarily for *causing* the abuse, but rather for not *disliking* it enough.}
  - *Spiritual*: neglect, and all of the above. *Any* abuse damages a child's spirit, or sense of hope; it does not have to be "the fear of God," although that certainly is included in the list.

Whatever form the abuse takes, it leaves marks on victims beyond the obvious. Abused children generally believe themselves somehow to be at fault. The resulting shame contributes to their belief of themselves as worthless and less-than – two traits that tend to follow them to adulthood. *See* **APPENDIX 4.**

Accountability: *the position in which one accepts full and complete responsibility for one's present and future, regardless of what has occurred in the past..*

A common trait among addicts is the shifting of blame to anyone but the self. "I wouldn't drink if you were nicer." "I'm an alcoholic because my parents were alcoholics." This does not mean that the statements are automatically false. For example, in my work with inmate addicts, I was often told that they came back to prison because their probation officer revoked them for (one example) "having a beer in the privacy of my own home." The statement is true; the accountability comes in (as it often did in my work with them) when they realize that, even if the probation officer is overly harsh, the inmate still did something he knew he was not allowed by the terms of his probation. As I said more times than I can recall, "You're not back here for doing it right. You don't get revoked for carrying an old lady's groceries, unless you carry them to your car instead of hers."

Accountability includes owning responsibility for our own thoughts and feelings. "You make me angry" is not only inappropriate, but also untrue. None of us has the ability/power/permission to make others feel the way we want them to; we can only trigger such responses. *See* **Emotions, Trigger.**

Addiction: *the continued use of a substance, person, or behavior, despite negative consequences.*

People have their own definitions for addiction, or at least their own relationships to it. For some, their addictive substance, person, or behavior makes things recognizable, okay, and meaningful. It is where they feel secure or normal, even when it's harmful. How many of us have preferred to be in a rocky relationship rather than in none at all? The unknown, the fear of being lonely, both contribute to continuing a harmful relationship.

Addiction develops partially due to the raising of tolerance one has to his drug of choice. *See* **Tolerance, Setpoint, APPENDIX 2,** *and* **APPENDIX 5.**

Affirmation: *a statement of praise, wisdom, or truth; an approving statement to the self from either the self or others.*

Repetition of affirmations can lead to re-training the brain toward acceptance of what is positive rather than dwelling on the negative, a trait common in addicts. See **Synapse.**

From my stay at Pia and Pat Mellody's Meadows in AZ, I learned not about affirmations, but also their power in overcoming beliefs that many, if not all, of us carry with us. The repetition of an affirmation, ten times ten times per day (thus 100 times daily), can produce a new synapse in the brain. I know this to be true, as I have practiced my affirmations over the twenty years since my stay at their facility. My all-time favorite affirmation is: *I am valuable in spite of my imperfections.* I tend these days, in fact, to believe I'm valuable *because* of them.

Aggression: *See* **Patterns of Behavior.**

Alcoholic: *a person addicted to alcohol. See* **Addiction.**

Alcoholics Anonymous: *a support program founded by Bill W. and Dr. Bob, two alcoholics who discovered that their recovery was not possible without the assistance and support of other alcoholics also working toward recovery, and the willingness to spread the message to other alcoholics.*

It is important to note that, despite what some devotees think, AA is not therapy. It is *therapeutic*, of course, just like exercise is, but it is a program run by its members without connection to any therapeutic model. It was designed by its originators to be a support program.

AA has given rise to a number of other similar programs; actually, they are programs that are based on the AA model, and they are too numerous to mention. No, that's not true – it's just that I don't know all of them well enough to avoid missing some, so I'll mention only a few – C(ocaine)(Addicts)A, N(arcotics)A, O(vereaters)A, and so on.

There are several **–Anon** groups, too, like Al-Anon, which is for families and friends of alcoholics. These are extremely important support groups for those whose lives are affected by addicts. They advocate the self-care necessary for those people. We cannot change the addicts in our lives; we can only protect ourselves from the ill-effects, which may include such drastic measures as kicking an addicted offspring out of the house, or leaving an addicted spouse. See **APPENDIX 6.**

Alienation: *isolation, separation, or estrangement from others.*

This happens to addicts, often beginning with their families, from whom addict separate and find others who do what they are doing. Most groups of addicts use at the same level; this way, they can say they do what "everyone else" does, and they are also no worse than others. See **Cop-out.**

Ambivalence: *the state of being "wishy-washy," or possessed at the same time by two contradictory emotions, beliefs, or desires.*

This generally occurs when the addict begins to realize that maybe their substance or behavior isn't quite as wonderful as it used to be. "Should I get clean or keep using?" This is also a state found in families and friends of addicts, who may not believe that "*MY* child/parent/friend/boss" could actually have a substance (or other) problem.

Amends: *the realization that you have done harm to another, and the face-to-face apology and acceptance of your responsibility for having done that harm.*

An amends may be accompanied by a statement of effort to avoid repetition of the harmful action. At the very least, that sentiment is implied.

Making amends is often difficult. There are times, however, when to do so is inappropriate, as when it would harm the injured party, who may, in fact, never want to lay eyes on you again. Part of recovery, nonetheless, is accepting the responsibility for inappropriate actions, even if making the amends is not possible. *See* **Accountability**

Anger: *Often confused with Rage, anger is a normal and protective emotion.*

A part of the foundation of rage. Anger is an emotion; rage is a *behavior*, recognizable immediately by destructive actions, loudness, violence and its threat, etc. Anger protects us and others and is a call to restorative action. Telling people they shouldn't feel anger is like telling them they shouldn't feel joy. *See* **Emotions, Fear, Shame, Rage.**

Attachment: *a bond, connection, or emotional tie between people resulting in attraction, dependence, or emotional satisfaction.*

This, of course, includes attachment to one's addiction.

Avoidance: *the choice to not deal with a particular situation (such as recovery), thus being unwilling or unable to change for the better.*

Avoidance can be practiced by procrastination, a "deaf ear," lack of self-knowledge or concern.

~ 𝔹 ~

BAC: *blood alcohol content.* The amount of alcohol in a person's blood. This is a function of the amount of alcohol, the amount of time it's present in the body, and the person's weight, with a difference between men and women due to differing body fat ratios between the two sexes. Sorry, ladies.

It's important to understand that BAC and *tolerance* are quite difference. BAC will remain constant per person while s/he is at the same weight. Tolerance may differ from one incident of drinking to the next. *See* **APPENDIX 1.**

Baggage: *basically, everything we have seen and done and been, and has been done to us, throughout our lives*

Sorting it all out is a help. An adult ed. student of mine once wrote an essay about a duffel bag his father had left him, which he used hitchhiking around the country. He wrote of how sometimes it weighed him down, and other times he was so glad to have it, it weighed almost nothing at all. I realized he had written a wonderful metaphor for men and their fathers, and all the advice (and perhaps subconscious learnings) that is passed down. Our baggage is what we carry with us; with strong boundaries, we may be able to sort out what we don't need and carry only what serves us.

Blackout: *that point at which a person's brain, while still functioning, is no longer capable of taking information into the part of the brain that holds memories.*

If you were to hypnotize a person who had a blackout, this would still not retrieve the memories of the time spent during the episode. The chemical interferes with the transfer of electrical signals between brain cells; in short, they simply never arrive. Most non-alcoholics will *pass out* prior to having a blackout, unless they are drinking quickly – an extremely dangerous activity, given the extreme shock to the inexperienced body. Twenty-one-shots-on-your-twenty-first-birthday? A very dangerous idea. *See* **Pass Out, Grey Out.**

Blame: *a defense mechanism that allows us to go through life without owning responsibility for anything we do, instead holding others responsible for everything that happens to us.*

Blame leads to victimhood, which will not allow recovery. For example: you're born into a family full of chefs. Your parents, grandparents, uncles, aunts, siblings, all are chefs. Clearly, you grow up in an atmosphere of chefs, with all the inherent vocabulary and other trappings. You, though, want to be an auto mechanic. However, being bright, you are seen to have the highest possibilities in cooking, so your parents send you to the finest chef school in the country. You do well, because that's what you do, and you graduate with the highest of honors. You leave the ceremony wearing your robe and chef hat, carrying your diploma in one hand and your spatula in the other. Across the street you see a man with his car hood up. Because you're helpful and, like most graduates, you think you can do anything, you approach the man and ask if you can help. "Please do," says the hapless driver, so you begin to poke around with your spatula, looking for something to flip. "What are you doing?" you're asked. "Helping you fix your car," you reply. "Well, I think you're an idiot," comes the retort, whereupon you smack the guy over the head with your spatula. The police are called, and you end up in jail. *Do you get to blame your parents because they sent you to chef school?*

Obviously not – but your background is clearly a *factor* in the decisions you made.

We don't get to blame others for our decisions, but we do get to acknowledge that factors in our childhoods may explain why certain things happened, and why we think the way we do. Another example, this one true. One of my former clients was part of the first family to move from Puerto Rico to a Maine town. He stated that growing up was tough; he faced a great deal of prejudice and was thus in many fights. I asked him if he blamed his parents for being Puerto Rican. He looked at me like I was crazy. I continued, "Well, this wouldn't have happened if they hadn't been Puerto Rican, would it?" We can't be blamed for the circumstances of our births, but they are factors in our lives, aren't they? *See* **Bu Hu, Defense Mechanisms,** and **Victim.**

Bottom: *the low point that we reach that convinces us, finally, that it's time to make changes.*

Warning: There are always more levels below "bottom." Without being pessimistic, things can always get worse. The key is deciding that a certain point is where we draw the line. It varies from person to person.

Bottom Line: *you aren't going to get into recovery because I change.*

Addicts often reject counselors because they (the addicts) don't agree with them (the counselors) or their (the counselors') suggestions. They (the addicts) still expect to be able to do it their (the addicts') way. Wrong answer!

Boundaries: According to Pia Mellody, Boundaries are *a system of limit-setting that enhance a person's sense of self while controlling the impact of reality on the self and others.*

What? Basically, strong boundaries initially are formed when a person has a strong sense of self. Who am I? Who is in charge of my life? Is my locus of control within me or without? The answers allow reality to be interpreted in that sense of self. "Bob likes the Yankees; I like the Red Sox. I am complete within these two views of reality and don't need to be threatened because Bob doesn't agree with me [even though he's an idiot if he doesn't!]"). I can either understand that Bob will always like the Yankees and choose to avoid him, or accept the fact and continue my relationship with him. Either way, I am no longer surprised by his point of view and can thus prepare myself for interactions with Bob.

Being able to set strong boundaries is one of the most important tools of recovery, both for addicts and for those who are involved with them.

Boundaries allow us to observe the behaviors of others without becoming a part of them (I don't have to like the Yankees because Bob does). Someone being disrespectful to me – that's not about me, but rather about that person, and I don't have to buy into what he's selling, or to let him "rent space in my head." If someone pushes my buttons, well, they're *my* buttons, and I can disconnect the power source.

One example I used often with inmate clients was to ask what their first strip-search was like. Most respond that it was terribly invasive, embarrassing, and uncomfortable. I would then ask what the *last* one was like. Most said it wasn't nearly as bad, just a "matter of course." When asked why this is so, most would say, "I got used to it." I think this is not quite true, and that they don't give themselves enough credit. A strip search will always be invasive; however, the men, without knowing they were doing so, simply altered the *value* of the search as it related to whatever else was going on (visits, random searches, etc.). They have set a boundary without realizing it.

Like anything, this is easier said than done, but strong boundaries are achievable through practice. See **Steve**.

Bu Hu: *an ancient Chinese philosophy developed by the Philosopher,* **Po Mee***, that promotes the idea that nothing is our fault, but is instead directly the result of circumstances, bosses, spouses (current and ex), dogs, ducks, the weather, traffic, Steve, etc., etc., etc..*

Those who subscribe to *Bu Hu* are able to go through their entire lives without taking responsibility for anything. In so doing, they never have to change anything or look at their own actions, and they live their lives content in the knowledge that there's nothing they can do to make any changes. Everything happens *to* them. See **Grandiose Thinking**.

Catharsis: *that wonderful moment when what needs to be realized is, in fact, realized.*

This is signified by an incredible release of emotion, of tension, of anxiety, and is often accompanied by tears.

Closure: *resolution: of relationships (with people, with addictions); the denouement, or end of the chapter (which allows the next to begin).*

When all the answerable questions have been answered, healing is possible, but certainly not automatic. With closure, the real work of recovery can begin.

Codependence: *an unhealthy attachment to another to the detriment of oneself, and the inability to set and maintain appropriate boundaries; taking responsibility inappropriately for the actions, thoughts, or feelings of others.*

Codependence is often characterized by caretaking, with the best intentions, of someone who is addicted or otherwise dysfunctional. For example: the difference between an alcoholic and a codependent? The smell. Or – are you familiar with Codependent Insurance? *MY* fault.

A codependent is often addicted to the addict. If I'm codependent, I blame myself for what you do, I make excuses for what you do, I think you'll get better if I behave myself, and I believe it my responsibility to make everything right.

Codependence is a disability to develop and maintain proper boundaries to protect oneself from the behaviors of others. "You ruined my day!" is likely the statement of a codependent.

The major problem with codependence is that it's the wrong thing done for the right reasons. It's the protection of the addict in order to keep him/her out of trouble, but at the same time it means there are no negative consequences for the addictive behaviors. The wife who calls in for her husband with "the flu" when he is actually too hung over to get out of bed is trying to protect him, but it, in fact, supports his negative behaviors.

Compliance: *the appearance of agreeing and cooperating with absolutely everything a counselor or therapist says in order to actually avoid doing the real work necessary.*

Counselors will often pray to be delivered from the compliant client. This is the client that will "tell 'em what they want to hear." This appearance of agreeableness allows the client to fall through the proverbial cracks and is a subtle form of resistance. *See* **Resistance.**

Constructive: *a less-judgmental term for "positive" or "right."*

Addicts are extremely sensitive to criticism, but tend to be a little more open to terms like this. *See* **Destructive.**

Contract: *an agreement between parent and child stating that if the child calls while under the influence, the parent will pick the child up and wait until the next day to discuss the matter, without punishment. Likewise, similar positive agreements between adults, often between counselor and client.*

Like it or not, our children are going to experiment. Far too many young people die each year from drug use, some of them because of fear of parental reaction – so they stay out instead of coming home, or ride in cars driven by intoxicated friends. Is there anything worse than the loss of a child when such loss could be prevented?

Coping mechanism: *learned ways of getting through stressful situations while maintaining consistency internally. These mechanisms may be conscious or unconscious.*

Some coping mechanisms may be *constructive,* such as leaving a problem alone for a while and coming back after a break. Leaving the problem and getting drunk, however, would be a *destructive* coping mechanism.

Cop-out: *basically, any excuse that prevents us from doing the work necessary.*

Cop-out is a slightly harsher tone to use with hard-core excusers, and counselors are advised to use it only if they have a strong rapport with their clients. It's effective for getting someone's attention.

Corporal punishment: *the use of force to discipline.*

Often justified by misquoting the Bible: "Spare the rod and spoil the child." This is the same rod that, with the *staff*, comforts those who walk through the Valley of the Shadow of Death; that is, the shepherd's crook. One proponent of spanking told me "First you spank the child, then you have a conversation with him about what he did wrong, then you hug him." I asked if the child understood the conversation. "Of course," she replied. "Then why do you have to hit him?" She added that one should never use one's hand to spank a child, so the hand doesn't hurt him. I can't believe a child wouldn't see whose hand is holding the switch. The other thing is – and this is from experience – when a child is being spanked, he's not thinking about what he did wrong; he's thinking of the great amount of pain he's experiencing from someone who is supposed to protect him. If corporal punishment is appropriate, why do so many of us feel guilty afterwards? *See* **Discipline**.

~ D ~

Defects of Character: *a term used by Anonymous programs as part of what they want their Higher Powers to remove from them.*

I have never liked this term, though I understand its use. I believe it to be something that fosters *shame*, which addicts already have in excess. Let's use resorting to drinking as an example. Little Johnny grows up in a dysfunctional family in which his basic needs are not met (that is, safety, security, nurturing, proper role modeling, etc.). He discovers that he gets those things when he drinks. Is his drinking a defect? I think not. It's a *survival tool*, the only one he has at the moment, since other coping mechanisms have not been taught to him. It's not a *good* tool, but it works, at least for the moment. So when Step 6 is expressed - We were entirely ready to have God remove all these defects of character – I much prefer the idea that we are ready to have God remove these *survival tools that are no longer appropriate.*

Defense mechanism: *a way of protecting the self from potential anxiety-producing awareness.*

The addict confronted by family and friends will often use denial, projection, anger, and other behaviors to avoid facing the truth. "I can handle it." "You should see that other guy." "*YOU* should talk! What about *your*…?" Examples: Blaming – Pointing to others as the cause of the behavior. ("I wouldn't drink so much if you would just quit nagging me.")

- Denial – Refusing to acknowledge that a problem exists. ("I could quit drinking whenever I want to – I just don't want to.")
- Isolation – Abandoning friends or family members in order to pursue one's addiction without being criticized or asked to stop.
- Minimizing – Attempting to downplay the severity of one's dependence upon alcohol. ("I only have one or two drinks to wind down after work. It's no big deal.")
- Maximizing – Making everything larger than they are. ("This is the worst thing that has ever happened to me!")
- Projection – Taking negative emotions one is feeling and assigning them to others, which some experts believe to be associated with paranoia. ("Everybody hates me!")
- Rationalization – Supplying reasons that "justify" one's unhealthy behavior. ("Hey, I don't want to drink so much, but it's the only way that I can deal with the pressures at work and still keep my job.")

Denial: *a much over-used category for those who are unwilling to address their issues; a way to forget or ignore such issues and thus avoid conscious awareness of problems.*

[Any who mention rivers when discussing this term should be taken out back and shot, in my humble and tolerant opinion.] Denial has become THE term for those in the pre-contemplative stage of awareness. In fact, it more often describes those who are not yet willing to accept treatment or help for their addiction.

Depressant: *a drug which lowers the body's ability to respond (lowers neurotransmission levels).*

This does *not* mean that if you take a depressant, you will become *depressed* (although it is possible). It means reflexes, thought processes, and bodily functions slow down.

Some depressants are prescribed for pain relief, and as sleeping aids.

Depressants include barbiturates, benzodiazepines, opioids, Suboxone, cannabis, and others (cannabis is also considered a narcotic and a hallucinogen).

Trick Question Time: Where does nicotine fall: depressant or stimulant?

Nicotine is actually an "all-arounder," which means it does both. Those who smoke tobacco know of that first cigarette "waker-upper," while they may also smoke to calm themselves down.

Effects of depressants can include lack of coordination, increased anxiety, pain relief, sedation, cognitive and memory impairment, euphoria, dissociation, muscle relaxation, lowered blood pressure/heart rate, respiratory depression, and death. See **APPENDIX 3.**

Destructive: *a polite and non-judgmental way to say "negative" or "wrong."*

"Your behavior is destructive" is a less-threatening than "You're wrong!" See **Constructive.**

Dialogue: *honest and genuine communication between oneself and others, or* inner *communication, involving active speaking and listening.*

Discipline: *a method of bringing up children by setting strong boundaries and sticking to them.*

Not many parents would say that children need no discipline. The screaming child in the supermarket is rarely looked upon with joy by either the parents or innocent bystanders. A child who throws a tantrum has learned that this is what helps him get his way; thus, the parent is responsible, and more discipline is needed (actually, starting from the beginning was needed).

Beating a child – okay, *spanking* a child – may work, briefly (if it were a permanent fix, it would only have to happen once, wouldn't it?), but I challenge what it teaches. It works well for parents who want their child to fear them, or to resent them. When a child is spanked, hit, or yelled at by those who are supposed to protect them, it's likely that the message is being lost because of the pain or fear. It's simple: if they're old enough to understand reason, then reason with them. If they're *not* old enough to understand reason, they won't understand why they're being spanked.

Drink: *One beer (12 oz.) = one normal glass of wine = one mixed drink (not – repeat – NOT including Long Island Ice Teas, etc. We're talking a normal drink with only 1 – 1 ½ oz. of alcohol).* See **APPENDIX 2.**

Drug of choice: *for the purposes of the Addictionary, this will refer not only to chemicals, but also behaviors and people to whom one may become addicted.*

Dry: *the status of a person who has simply stopped using his/her substance/behavior/person of choice, without the necessary steps involved with gaining understanding of why the addiction existed in the first place.*

There are some who manage to give up their addiction simply by strength of their will alone. Without addressing the underlying factors involved in addiction, addicts tend to carry the effects of those factors without change. These people are referred to as being *dry drunks* (in the case of alcoholics, though the term can be used with all addictions). People who are dry tend to be miserable, unpredictable, with something to prove to others. See **Recovery, Sober.**

DWI/DUI/OUI: (Driving While Intoxicated, Driving Under the Influence, Operating Under the Influence) *a charge leveled against those who operate their vehicles after having overused their drug of choice.*

In most states, .08 is the level at which a person can be charged with this offense. Often, there are efforts to lower the level to .05, but this is often defeated on the grounds that it will adversely affect not the chronic alcoholic who drives often under the influence, but rather the "occasional" over-user who drives while intoxicated.

In actuality, the occasional user is *more* dangerous than the chronic user, as the novice generally does not have the tolerance of the chronic user and is thus more likely to be out of control. This of course, does not make the chronic user safe; this is a relative issue. See **Tolerance, BAC, APPENDICES 1 & 2.**

Dysfunction: *the inability to act appropriately with others or the self in whatever roles one's relationships and life arenas might be.*

Addicts are dysfunctional; so are their children. It can be assumed that no one is fully functional, despite the assertions of my first two wives. Full functionality probably doesn't exist, but we can get closer by gaining as much self-knowledge as we can. Part of functionality is coming to the realization that we are responsible for our own lives; blaming others is a sign of dysfunction.

~ E ~

Education: *what this **Addictionary** is all about.*

You can find out any information you want about any drug online. Wikipedia has been used for some of the information in this booklet. Sometimes, though, what is more helpful than formal definition is the way a term is used in real life. Defining *addiction* does not come close to explaining it. *Addictionary* is designed to bring the terminology to life and understanding as much as possible.

Emotions: *feelings; things which addicts often try to avoid/ignore/deny.*

Nobody can make us feel, or think, anything. If we think that this statement is not true, then we are giving power over us to others.

Pia Mellody developed a list of seven core feelings, out of which all others are formed. To help learn the core emotions, just remember J-P-FLAGS.

Core Emotions

Joy
Pain
Fear
Loneliness
Anger
Guilt
Shame

Many people see this as a negative list, with *joy* being the only positive feeling. In fact, the emotions are simply emotions; it's what we *do* with them that makes them positive or negative. Each feeling has burdens when unacknowledged, and gifts when we are aware of them. Addicts tend not to be aware of their feelings, or they try to hide from them. Rather than a page with 70 cute emoticons on it, this list can be much simpler and straight-forward.

Core Emotions	Burdens	Gifts
Joy	Hysteria, Chaos	Hope, Healing, Spirituality
Pain	Hopelessness	Healing, Growth
Fear	Panic, Paranoia, Cockiness	Wisdom, Protection
Loneliness	Isolation	Reaching Out
Anger	Rage	Strength, Energy, Motivation
Guilt	Immobility	Values, Amends
Shame	Worthlessness	Humility, Humanity

Core Emotions	Common words associated with the core emotions
Joy	Happy, glad, pleased, content, relieved, well, ducky, (really!), etc.
Pain	Hurt, sad, depressed, down, crummy, blue, remorseful, regretful, etc.
Fear	Scared, frightened, terrified, wary, "I don't trust him," "Watch out," etc.
Loneliness	Abandoned, etc.
Anger	Mad, ripped, pissed, furious, irate, emphatic, annoyed, irritated, etc.
Guilt	Sorry, apologetic, remorseful, regretful
Shame	Worthless, no-good, evil, a waste of air, etc.

The earlier we can recognize and consciously acknowledge each emotion, the better we can learn to avoid the burdens they bring. If I recognize anger when it is still simply anger, then the rage that has been my affliction for a huge portion of my life is not reached, because I know how to handle the anger.

This list certainly seems simplistic. Some counselors give clients a paper with seventy little faces on them with seventy emotions (one such list includes "Eavesdropping." *Really?*). Imagine being an addict, going for years without acknowledging your feelings, then being given a list of seventy and then being asked, "How does that make you feel?" By knowing how all of the seventy on that page fit into the core emotions, it not only simplifies the recognition of how you're feeling, but also allows the acknowledgement of them before they grow into the more dangerous burdens. For example, let's say I'm irritated. What is the core emotion of irritation? Anger. So I call it anger, and its recognition allows me to deal with it rather than stuffing it (can you relate, men?).

Men tend to stuff their emotions. Something happens at work, and we don't acknowledge it (because we're supposed to be tough, aren't we, guys?). So we push it deep down. Then we go home and when our sweetie asks how our day was, we blow up at her, and she catches all the emotion that has built up during the day. On the other hand, if we recognized the initial emotion when it occurred in the first place, then it's gone at that moment, and we go home and answer, "well, the day was a little tough, but I handled it."

I've been told that Pia and crew *love* has been added to the list of emotions. My opinion that it doesn't belong on the list comes from a belief that love encompasses *ALL* of the original core feelings, both burdens and gifts. I'm inclined now to think of love as a behavior. *See* **Feelings, Thoughts.**

Empathy: *the ability to understand not exactly how others feel, but rather to understand that they are feeling something.*

Can a man empathize with a woman in the transition phase of childbirth? Most will say "No," but it is possible. To say, "Gosh, Darling, I know just how you feel!" is not empathy, and such a statement is likely to cause great pain, along with a nasty divorce. However, to say something like "That must really be painful; you're doing great," while not a guarantee of success (transition is, after all, transition), is likely to be more acceptable.

I have had several kidney stones. I've been told by women who have experienced both labor and kidney stones that kidney stones are worse. I must say, though, that I would never *dream* of saying "I know just how you feel" – or, worse – "That doesn't hurt as much as my kidney stones, so get over it" to a woman in transition (how many of *you* would?).

"I know how you feel" is a statement that rarely works; nobody know *exactly* how someone else feels, even under identical circumstances. "That must be..." works much better. It validates the person's emotion and allows the attention to stay on the comforted rather than the comforter. "Oh, you'll get over it" is not a good example of empathy; neither is relating your own experience. Often (**men, pay attention**), it is the simple act of *listening*.

Empowerment: *a lovely occurrence that signifies the acceptance of one's own worth, strength, and capabilities.*

Empowerment is something difficult for many to achieve, much less understand. Feelings of shame inhibit the process. *This is not to be confused with accepting powerlessness over one's addiction.* By understanding that no one can control the effects of addiction, one can regain (or gain for the first time) power over one's own life.

Note: *power over the lives of other people is generally not regarded as a goal of recovery.*

Enabling: *the excusing of an addict's behaviors by those around him, which reinforces his negative behaviors.*

Enabling is one of the major obstacles to someone getting into recovery, as it keeps the addict from experiencing the negative effects of his addiction. The wife who calls her husband's work to tell them he has the "flu" when, in fact, he's hungover, allows him to continue this behavior without its consequences. This is usually done out of love and concern, but it pushes him deeper into his addiction.

Esteem: *positive regard.*

Addiction is noted as a disease of low self-esteem. An addict uses to escape the pain of his feelings of shame and lack of worth.

There are two types of esteem. The first is generally notable by its *tangible* attributes. People are proud of their children, their jobs, their cars, their sweeties, their clothing, and so on. This is *Other Esteem*. There is nothing wrong with having other esteem, except that it generally has little to do with the person who has it. We all too often will boost ourselves by what we have – our fancy house, those things on the previous list, which generally are things we can easily lose. *Self-esteem*, on the

other hand, consists of those things we have worked to build in ourselves – not our jobs, but the way in which we *do* them; not our spouses, but the depth of our love for them.

An exercise I use with clients is to have them name things of which they are proud, and I write them on the board. The guidelines are as follows: I am the judge of what I allow on the board, and no one is allowed to use something already used by another client. I always go last. One man said, "My heritage (he was Native American)." I disallowed it, much to his initial dismay. "You had no control over that," I explained, adding that that was also why I didn't allow intelligence, eye-color, and other born-with characteristics.

It often took over ten minutes for as many men to come up with one thing they honored in themselves. Interestingly, it would have taken half the time to come up with something they *didn't* like about themselves. Part of recovery is learning how to be a little gentler with the self, which means allowing self-esteem to grow. There is no shortage of people willing to point out our faults, including ourselves. Recognizing our positive qualities is not only not bragging, but also healthy. If I didn't think I could present the terms in this *Addictionary* well, I wouldn't be doing it.

Externalization: *a coping mechanism whereby one believes outside influences to have caused what has occurred due to what is within the individual.*

This is seen by people blaming others and their failure to take responsibility for their own present circumstances, behaviors, emotions, and beliefs. See **Bu Hu**.

~ 𝔉 ~

Falling Off the Wagon: *starting to drink again after being in recovery.*

An inaccurate term. Nobody *falls* off the wagon. Nobody drinks or uses again by accident. People *JUMP* off the wagon. It's all about accountability and taking responsibility for our actions. See **Slip.**

Fear: *an emotion that men often cannot admit to having.*

Men, in particular, move so quickly from fear to rage that they don't acknowledge that they have felt it. Part of Rage's foundation, fear is a natural part of us all. If we say, "Don't trust that guy," aren't we dealing with fear? Fear of what he may do, of how he may somehow throw a stone into the calm waters of our existence. I would ask inmate clients if they feared of any guards. They would say they didn't; but why, then, did they do what guards told them to do? Because they would lose privileges if they didn't. The stone in the calm waters of existence.

Was Muhammad Ali afraid of Joe Frazier? Most will answer, "No," but I can prove that he most certainly was, and I'll get no argument. How do I know he was afraid? Simple. He *trained*, and he did so with men who fought like Frazier. He was afraid of being punched by a man who could knock down a building, and he'd have been crazy *not* to have been. See **Emotions, Rage.**

Feedback: *the process by which we can tell others how we feel regarding their behaviors while avoiding being judgmental. Also, the process by which we can receive others' feelings about our behaviors.*

This is often mistakenly called "constructive criticism." In my opinion, while criticism can be used positively, it comes in a poor second to feedback. *Constructive criticism* usually sounds something like: "You're doing a good job [wait for it!], **but**..." It's the "but" that kills, that tends to undo whatever good will was brought by the initial praise.

There are many forms for giving feedback. I favor the following, from Pia Mellody: "When you ----- [describe behavior], what I make up about that is ---- [share your feeling], and I feel ---- [give the feeling].

For example: When you interrupt me, what I make up about that is that you don't care what I have to say, and I feel anger. This *may* be followed by a request to change the behavior, and it may not.

The other half of feedback is receiving it. Defending the behavior is inappropriate at this point; after all, the person has risked your anger/defensiveness to tell you something important. The appropriate immediate response is to think about what the person as said. The best answer is "Thank you."

Feedback is another's response to something you do. You are under no obligation to change that behavior, though it's certainly an option. It may depend on who is giving you the feedback. When my supervisor gives me feedback, I tend to think strongly about changing my behavior.

A key part of feedback is knowing the difference between observation and judgment. Feedback is based on observation rather than judgment, and most people believe they actually know the difference. Usually, they are mistaken. When I ask clients to make observations about my behavior, and then I pace, exhaling loudly and hitting my fist into my hand, they will often "observe" that I'm angry or stressed. These are *not* observations; they are judgments. The observations would be my pacing, exhaling loudly, and hitting my fist into my hand. In fact, when doing this demonstration, while I am showing signs usually connected to anger, I'm not angry; rather, I'm demonstrating it without actually being angry. See **S.O.S.**

Feelings: *Emotions, often confused with thoughts.*

Whenever you hear "I feel like...," understand that you're about to hear a thought. "I feel like it's going to rain" is not a feeling; it's a thought. " "I feel wonderful" is an emotion, a feeling. Not to be too nit-picky about it. See **Thoughts.**

Free Will: [Not to be confused with **Free Willy**.] *Something your children believe they have when it comes to what they do with their own bodies. Likewise, an excuse for our own inappropriate behavior.*

This point is inarguable. The best we can hope to do, as parents, is to educate our children to the best of our abilities and be there for them when the screw things up, as they will (as we did, didn't we?). They are going to experiment, and they won't call you before they do to ask for your permission. This is the time that is critical for role-modelling and over-seeing them.

Free Will is also a major excuse for our own self-harming behaviors. We often say (arrogantly) that it's our body, we can do what the hell we want, and we ignore the impact our behaviors may have on those who love us. *See* **Contract, Education.**

- G -

Genuineness: *that quality in people, and in this particular case, counselors, that indicates positive regard and respect for others (clients), which involves understanding the "point of origin" of the other person (in other words, where the person is coming from).*

Basically, what this means is that a counselor is "real." She is honest, sincere, and relating to clients honestly, not following learning points from a book.

In a shelter in which I once counseled, the men with whom I was working progressed to the point that they were able to give non-threatening feedback to others and themselves, including a proper acknowledgement of their feelings. My supervisor approached me and, in all sincerity, suggested that I ask my clients how they're doing "as if they're a car." "Excuse me?" I responded. "You know; 'I got up this morning and am only running on three cylinders.'" Immediately, visions of windshield wipers, seat adjustments, oil changes, and air conditioning went through my head. "That's interesting," I respectfully replied and thought nothing more about it until he brought it up again at a later time.

It might have been a perfectly reasonable way to elicit feelings, asking grown men how they felt by how they relate to being a car (I don't really believe that, though. Do you?). In this case, though, these men were already responding appropriately, every morning in group, to the rational and carefully addressed issues of their feelings. To introduce this other technique would have meant insulting men who had already progressed well beyond so simple a method, and it would have been incredibly non-genuine to the clients with whom I had developed a respectful rapport.

[I told this same supervisor at a later date that I had a client with poor circulation in his ankles. "You know what he needs," my supervisor said. "No, what?" I asked. "Suppository hose!" came the (triumphant?) response. "I don't think that'll work," I told him. "Why not?" "I don't think shoving his socks up his butt will help his ankles." He looked at me blankly. "*Support* hose," I said. "Oh," he replied; then, "*Ohhhhhhh.*" I was relieved of my position shortly thereafter. Perhaps I was *too* genuine.]

Grandiose Thinking: *a common state of addicts, and others, in which we believe ourselves to be the center of the universe; everything is about me.*

This is right in line with victim-thinking as well as the idea that we're better than anyone else. What is perhaps a surprising element of this is when we wonder, "How could God do this to me?", as if God has nothing better to do than single us out for punishment. This can also be the result of spoiling children.

Grey Out: *a minor black out. Memories can come back when we're reminded of activities. See* **Blackout, Pass Out***.*

Guilt: *the acceptance of responsibility for an inappropriate action, usually to another.*

If I offend you, and I offer no apology, our relationship, at best, will be *immobile*. That is, we will not progress, and your ability to trust me will diminish. If, however, I offer the appropriate response – "I'm sorry" – then we can move forward, and I have learned one of your *values* (whatever I did that was offensive), and made the *amends* I have offered you in my apology. See **Emotions, Amends.**

Guilt and Shame, Difference Between: *Guilt is an appropriate response to our doing something inappropriate. Shame is what we call ourselves when we've done so.*

People often confuse the two different emotions, but looked at in this way, it's really quite simple. If I step on your foot, it's appropriate for me to feel sorry for having done so (and in the best of worlds, I realize it and apologize). That's guilt. The shame happens immediately afterwards, when I walk away saying to myself, "What a clumsy fool I am." The shame is unnecessary, as long as the apology or amends has been delivered. See **Emotions, Shame, Fear, Anger.**

~ H ~

Hallucination: *a perception in the absence of external stimulus that has the qualities of real perception.*

Hallucinations are vivid, substantial, and are seen to be located in external objective space. They can occur in any sensory modality. See **APPENDIX 3** *for this and the next term.*

Hallucinogens: *psychoactive agents which can cause hallucinations.*

Examples include Ketamine®, phencyclidine, mescaline, LSD, and psilocybin ('shrooms). Pot is also a hallucinogen when used in a high enough quantity. Don't argue with me on this one; I know.

Higher Power: *an entity greater than oneself, often referred to as "God," but not necessarily one and the same.*

The reason to consider acknowledging a power greater than ourselves is to gain the awareness that **we are not in control**. It does not have to be religious. I tell my clients that when they are caught in an undertow, that's a power greater than themselves, and they'd better learn to work with it if they want to get the hell out of the water alive.

Homeostasis: *the body's ability (and need) to maintain balance, and to return to balance (or setpoint) after a challenge of some sort.*

This is the body's ability to return to rest after exertion, or sobriety after drinking. For example, in the case of alcohol, a depressant, the body has to pay attention to the lowering of function in order to allow the person to continue to function). If a person becomes an alcoholic, and thus has alcohol constantly in his system, his body has to work harder to maintain the *balance* of his regular life. His heart, his liver, and so on, all work harder, are under more stress, and thus the person is at higher risk of other physical problems. When the organs are working extra hard to maintain functioning, and the alcohol is suddenly withdrawn, the organs are *still* working at an increased pace, which is why sudden withdrawal from alcohol is potentially fatal without medical intervention. *See* **Setpoint**.

How does that make you feel? *A well-meaning but inappropriate question counselors love to ask and clients hate to hear.*

The question implies that other people or events can *make* us feel things, or think things, when, in fact, they can only *trigger* our feelings and thoughts. To ask people how something or someone "makes" them feel is to encourage them to avoid taking responsibility for their lives. A more appropriate question would be, "*How do you feel about that?*"

~ I ~

Inferiority: *a feeling (under the heading of SHAME) of being less-than; low self-esteem.*

One of the symptoms — and perhaps one of the causes — of addiction. The user resorts to his addiction to escape these feelings of not measuring up, of not being enough. Usually it is the result of some form of childhood trauma, often abuse, which does not allow the child to develop a sense of belonging. The drug of choice, and the using crowd, helps to dispel the low esteem.

Inner child: *that spirit of innocence that many believe to still exist within all adults, often lost through childhood trauma. English teachers will call such trauma the* loss of innocence. *It's usually replaced by tools necessary for the survival of adulthood.*

The above is nice in theory. However, in the cases of the majority of addicts, the inner child gets lost. Worse, in the case of abuse, the resulting adult may take over for the abuser after his abuser departs. This is all part of the low self-esteem and shame with which the child grows up.

Victims of abuse often blame themselves for what they experienced, believing that they "should have been able to prevent it or stop it." Not very likely, when an adult is the abuser. Also, they begin to believe they *deserve* such treatment. Many of my inmate clients related being *a bad kid*. How does a child become bad?

Attention paid to the inner child can result in a serenity heretofore not experienced by the recovering addict. While many might poo-poo the idea (how's that for an inner-child term?), others find it extremely rewarding when they can finally acknowledge the child who was not to blame for the victimization experienced during the growing up years.

The inner-child still finds the beauty in the world, in other people, and can react with joy to each dawning day. Oddly enough, recognition of one's inner child might just be a sign of maturity.

Insecurity: *lack of self-confidence and assurance; low self-esteem; feeling less-than, unworthy, not-enough.*

The basis of almost every addiction, often covered by overconfidence, bullying, and the inability to recognize areas that may need some work. Recovery depends upon at least some repair of this damage.

Instant Gratification: *the immediate pleasure received from the addictive substance/behavior/person.*

Addicts don't use to take care of tomorrow. They want it, they want it all, and they want it NOW.

Intervention: *a gathering of concerned individuals for the loving and supportive confrontation of an addict. The goal is that the addict will rehabilitation. Also, a television program of the same name which chronicles such activities.*

It is suggested that people connected to addicts watch this excellent television show. It documents the need for concerned "affected others" to take care of themselves and establish firm and clear boundaries around the addict's behavior. These include cutting off funding, cutting off housing, refusing to communicate when the addict is under the influence, etc. This type of intervention is extremely difficult and painful (trust me!), and it may seem like you're turning your back on your loved one. However, it is necessary, because you're of no help to your addict, or to anyone else in your family, if you're being held hostage by addictive behaviors.

Intimacy: *contrary to popular belief, this does not apply to the sexual nature of a relationship; rather, it is the ability to communicate with another purely and completely, or that level to which one is able to do so. It involves the ability to be familiar, open, and empathic.*

It Depends: *the beginning of a great many answers to specific questions.*

Far too many questions have automatic responses without taking into account specific circumstances. *See* **Trigger Responses.**

~ J ~

Journal: *to write in a dedicated manner of events that are seen as important by the writer/journalist.*

This is particularly helpful as one is entering the process of recovery as it documents the daily growth and changes in thinking that occur. The recovery process is impossible without such changes; thus, journaling allows for the evidence of growth. Many rehabilitation programs require journaling as a daily practice.

Joy: *an emotion often mistakenly seen as positive; it is positive when we make it so.*

When people believe joy to be positive, they ignore the negative things that can happen as a result of it. For example: we get a raise, then decide we need to celebrate by partying. We party too hearty, drink too much, then, as we drive home we get pulled over for an OUI. So much for joy. Yes, we *like* joy, but we still need to attend to what we do when we experience it. In the 1990's I pitched a perfect game in men's slow-pitch (12-foot arc) softball. Afterwards, someone offered me a beer. I declined – why would I want to drink a depressant when I was feeling so much joy? *See* **Emotions.**

Judgments: *things often confused with* **observations.**

When we're asked to make an observation about something, we often will give judgments. This is a critical error when giving someone feedback or when involved in an S.O.S. *See* **Feedback, Observation, S.O.S.**

– L – There is no – K – So sue me.

Loneliness: *an emotion with a serious message.*

When we feel loneliness, the message is that we need to contact somebody. For many, isolation is one of the symptoms of impending relapse, telling us that we need to reach out to someone. *See* **Emotions.**

Lumber Therapy: *an innovative, highly effective, and absolutely unethical model of counseling that involves a counselor hitting his/her client over the head with a 2x4 to gain the attention necessary to proceed in recovery.*

– M –

Mystique of Pot: *many people believe pot is not harmful, that no one was ever killed by a pot-smoking driver, that pot is "good for you."*

Cannabis is a drug. **It won't stop being a drug because you want to keep smoking it**. THC (tetrahydrocannabinol), its active ingredient, has the power to affect our thinking even while we are enjoying its calming effects.

It also has the power to produce psychiatric breakdowns in some people. It is also a gateway drug for some people (if it wasn't for you, that doesn't mean it isn't for others. Alcohol has yet to be addictive for me, yet I'm fully aware that it is highly addictive).

Pot has something like 45 unidentified chemicals in it. When it's lit on fire, that number grows to something like 435.

"Yeah, but it's *natural!!*" True – but, again, when you light a match to it, the chemical reaction brings about changes that make it no longer natural. You can also say that poppies are natural; after various chemical changes, though, we end up with heroin and morphine.

Only relatively recently has law enforcement been testing for pot and other chemicals during drunk driving incidents. There are those who swear that they drive better when smoking pot. Pot does, in fact, enable one to concentrate more when using it. *However*, that focus extends pretty much to one task at a time; throw something else into the mix – like fiddling with the radio, eating, and at the same time staying on the road – well, that's when problems arise.

Anyone who has ever smoked (at least good shit) knows the delay that occurs in response time; after all, that's part of the fun, isn't it?

The following is from a study by Leirer VO, Yesavage JA, and Morrow DG.

> This study finds evidence for 24-h carry-over effects of a moderate social dose of marijuana on a piloting task. In separate sessions, nine currently active pilots smoked one cigarette containing 20 mg of delta 9 THC and one Placebo cigarette. Using an aircraft simulator, pilots flew just before smoking, and 0.25, 4, 8, 24, and 48 h after smoking. Marijuana impaired performance at 0.25, 4, 8, and 24 h after smoking. While seven of the nine pilots showed some degree of impairment at 24 h after smoking, only one reported any awareness of the drug's effects. The results support our preliminary study and suggest that very complex human/machine performance can be impaired as long as 24 h after smoking a moderate social dose of marijuana, and that the user may be unaware of the drug's influence.

There are many who believe in the legalization of pot. There is no easy answer to this. People smoke it because of the psychological effect it has, then say that effect isn't there when they want to drive their cars. You can't have it both ways. *If they legalize your drug of choice, will your decisions be any less foolish when you're under the influence of it?* The problem with legalizing pot is that there are some who will be unable to moderate their use. There's no doubting its medicinal value, but recreational use comes with accompanying dangers. A word to the wise…

~ N ~

Narcissism: *excessive preoccupation with oneself; viewing the world through one's own mirror, if you will.*

From the Greek myth. Narcissus fell in love with his own reflection. A common phrase heard by and told to such people is "Not everything is about *you!*" Such people view the world in terms of what they believe they've done for it. Sometimes known as trumpism (all right, I'm sorry, but I just *had* to throw that in there). (I'm not really sorry).

Narcotics: *Originally referred medically to any psychoactive compound with sleep-inducing properties; now associated more with opiates and opioids.*

Opiates include morphine, heroin, and derivatives such as oxy- and hydrocodone.

Nature versus Nurture: *the never-ending battle of whether conditions come from ourselves or from those around us; inheritance or environment?*

The difficulty in answering this question is that science is forever coming up with new research favoring one or the other side. It's also a convenient way of holding on to blame for the difficulties in or resistance to the hard work of recovery. "I can't help it, I was *born* this way," or, "It's not my fault; my parents taught me this way," or, "I came from a bad neighborhood."

Ultimately, does it matter *how* we get to these places in our lives? However we get there, we can't go and ask our parents to retrain us, nor can we return to the womb of a different mother to be re-gestated. The burden of change lies with us and *only* with us.

~ O ~

Observation: *the relating of what is seen without deciding what it means.*

This is a key factor in feedback and the S.O.S. "The sky is blue" is an observation. "It's a nice day" is a judgment. *See* **Feedback, Judgment, S.O.S.**

~ P ~

Pain: *an emotion that informs us that something is wrong and needs attention.*

When we hurt, physically, this is not a negative; it's a sign that we need to take care of something. If we don't do something, whatever is wrong could get much worse. Emotionally, the same thing can happen. When we're in pain, we need to do something. If we stuff it, or ignore it, the pain can lead to depression and hopelessness, which, in turn, lead people to potential drug use or other inappropriate methods of handling it. *See* **Emotions.**

Passing Out: *losing consciousness due to excess alcohol (or other chemical) in the body. NOT TO BE CONFUSED WITH* **Blackout.**

Most inexperienced drinkers will pass out (due to their lower levels of tolerance) before blacking out. Leave someone drunk alone, he falls asleep. *See* **Blackout, Grey Out.**

Patterns of Behavior/Communication: *the ways in which we tend to respond to certain stimuli.*

These tend to be learned responses which, with work, can be changed to give us a more positive way of living in our respective worlds. It can be argued (indeed, I've argued it myself in countless group sessions dealing with this issue) that there is only one truly appropriate pattern of behavior as discussed below. This does not mean that anyone, myself included, always responds appropriately; only that knowledge is power and can help us change destructive behaviors.

- ❖ **Passive:** allowing others to impose their wills on us. We bend to the beliefs of others, we don't make waves, and we rarely get things our way (terminal victimhood). The danger is that we let things build up inside us until there is no more room, whereupon we buy high-powered rifles, climb to the tops of water towers, and shoot at anyone that moves. A less-extreme example is the senior McFly in the first of the *Back to the Future* movies, although we tend to see his explosion (hitting Biff) as a positive step. Passive: *I don't matter; you do.*

- ❖ **Passive-Aggressive:** an oft-misunderstood term, this refers to the subtle control of others through psychological means, including sarcasm, procrastination, and the like. It is hostility masked by agreeability. *I matter; you don't, but I'm not going to tell you, at least not openly.*

- ❖ **Aggressive:** another oft-misunderstood term. Aggressive behaviors are used without regard for the rules. It's win-at-all-costs. Even wars have rules, and we tend to get up-in-arms (pun intended) when one side battles without regard for those rules.

    Almost every coach will tell players, "Get out there and be aggressive." Is this what they truly mean? Football players are penalized for clipping, for illegal hits to vulnerable opponents. These are clearly aggressive moves. I argue that boxing is not an aggressive sport, but rather an assertive one. Biting the opponent's ear is aggressive; hitting him below the belt is aggressive. We don't like any of those tactics. Knocking the opponent out, though, is clearly within the rules. Also, all participants know and accept the rules. I have yet to see a fight in which a boxer returns to his corner after a few seconds to complain, "Hey, did you see that? That guy's trying to *hit* me!"

    Do we expect coaches to change their language? Absolutely not; but if what they truly desire in their players are the aggressions shown above, then they will not be popular among fans. Playing within the rules of the particular activity, whether it's boxing, arguing, war, whatever, will see no examples of aggressive behavior. None of these rules seem to apply in hockey. Aggressive: *I matter, you don't matter, and I'm definitely going to let you know.*

- ❖ **Assertive:** this is the behavior that works within the realm of respect for other and for the rules of the activity at hand. It is marked by self-respect, which, by its very nature, extends respect to others (what truly self-respecting person needs to make life difficult for anyone else?). It involves setting clear, respectful boundaries and sticking to them. Assertive: *I matter, you matter.*

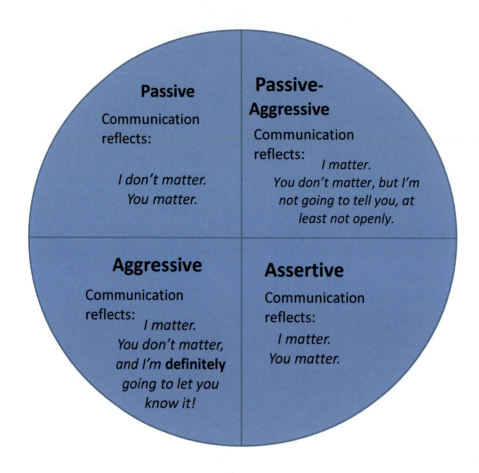

Personal Growth: *the process of getting to know oneself better, conquering demons, self-actualizing, growing in recovery, etc., which generally results in increased self-confidence and serenity, among other fine things.*

Recovery is all about Personal Growth.

Poly-drug use: *having more than one drug of choice; using more than one drug at a time.*

This brings up the danger of using more than one drug at a time. While it may make logical sense to use a depressant to come off the effects of a stimulant, to do so is dangerous, because there is *never* a guarantee that the expected effects will occur. This is why your pharmacist keeps a record of your medications, in case your prescribed drugs have contraindications when used together.

This is something to warn your children about. Many people use alcohol and cannabis at the same time. This provides an additional danger than simply the combination of two drugs. Pot is a central nervous system depressant. One of its uses, medicinally, is for people who are undergoing chemotherapy – pot suppresses the gag-reflex, allowing these people to keep their food down. If we drink and smoke pot at the same time, we reduce our body's natural protective reflex, i.e., regurgitating the excess alcohol (toxic to our systems), and thus open the door to alcohol poisoning and, perhaps, death.

PrisonThink: *a way of thinking without fully exploring consequences; this often leads to time behind bars (and not the ones in which we drink).*

Prison is the answer to questions we don't know we're asking. "Should I take this car?" *Prison.* "Should I beat up this guy who richly deserves it for insulting my Sweetie?" *Prison.* "Should I go ahead and drive because I can handle my liquor?" *Prison.* Get it?

Projection: *the fine art of perceiving one's negative qualities in others so as not to have to deal with them yourself. "No one should eat cucumbers; I don't like them."*

Projection is practiced among those new to recovery. Since they are embracing new and helpful techniques for living, they often decide that others have the same affliction from which they are now in recovery. I faced this often; I am not a recovering chemical addict (there is more than one way to skin that cat), so my moderate drinking habits (one drink per day, usually, with dinner) was often used to accuse me of being in denial. This is understandable: "why can he drink if I can't?" That's simply the way things are, even though it just doesn't seem fair, does it?

~ R ~

Rage: *In the model proposed by Pia Mellody, Rage is the combination of anger, fear, and shame.*

Anger gets really bad press, and some models say that anger must be eliminated. Nothing could be further from the truth. If you witness an injustice to someone, anger is the natural response. What we *do* with that anger is where care must be taken. Let's say someone cuts you off when you're driving. What's your first response? Most will say *anger*, proving it by the raised finger of indignation. I offer that the first feeling is *fear*: that idiot could have killed you. The anger and shame follow, so quickly that many (perhaps mostly men?) don't even know they've arisen. The *shame?*

Perhaps that the person didn't respect your right to safety on the road, or perhaps it's the subsequent possible loss of your control.

I like this model. As a recovering rager myself (Intermittent Explosive Disorder), it has fueled my recovery and made not only my life easier, but also the lives of those with whom I interact. *See* **Emotions.**

Rationalization: *a defense mechanism which enables one to excuse inappropriate behaviors.* "Everybody *smokes pot these days.*"

Recovery: *a process by and through which one not only ceases one's addictive behaviors/uses, but also addresses the underlying causes of the addiction. See* **Rehabilitation.**

Though there are certainly people who have given up their substance/behavior/person without going through a great deal of work, most get into recovery by hitting bottom, whatever that is for each individual, and feeling the pain that addiction has brought to them and others. A great many people who can simply stop tend to refuse to acknowledge that such an act may be impossible for others, and they may lack the compassion necessary to understand the pain and hard work it takes for most to develop a good, strong recovery program.

I have come to believe that recovery is the discovery that I still have much to learn.

Rehabilitation: *a formal process by which one learns to replace addictive or other behaviors with appropriate coping and survival skills.*

It is perfectly understandable that so many people fear going to rehab. After all, it means that most of what we have based our life on up to this point is – the temptation is to say "wrong," which makes the whole idea of rehab more difficult. Thus we go with – *destructive*. That may be an easier term to swallow. It means being completely open and honest, risking condemnation from others because, after all, no one has had it as bad as we have, nor have they done the horrible things we have done. It means coming face to face with the shame that has been so strong a cause of our dysfunction in the first place.

My own experience of rehab meant the initial acceptance of the fact that I had a great deal of work to do, that my life was out of control (Holy Cow! That sounds suspiciously like Step One!), and that I had no clue as to how to fix things.

What made my process a bit more difficult was that when I went to rehab, I had already worked for years as a Masters Level counselor. I knew a whole lot of shit, let me tell you, and I was pretty good at it, if my students and clients could be believed.

The first thing my personal counselor told me was: "This is going to be difficult for you." "Why?" I asked her. "Because you know what we're doing. I want you to forget everything you know and let us handle things." When I did so – the third day – my recovery process began.

It's important to realize that rehabilitation may come with a cost. When a person experiences the rehabilitative process, it may mean that relationships *will* change, and some will need to be relinquished.

Many relationships are built on dysfunction. Alcoholics and enablers are a perfect match, but when the alcoholic enters recovery (is rehabilitated), what is there for the enabler to enable? It doesn't mean that the partner has become bad or evil, just that the reason for the relationship no longer exists. If this is so, why stay in it? Divorce is a frequent result of rehab, but usually the partners end up better off (*if* the both choose to be responsible for their own happiness).

Think of relationships as a dance: each partner's movements depend on the other's movements (okay, maybe not *all* dances). When one partner learns new and better steps, if the other can't keep up, there is no dance.

Consider a relationship as being a pair of clasped hands: two addicts, addict and enabler, whatever, each has a purpose within the relationship.

One of the partners enters into recovery. The relationship between the two now changes: the partner on the left enters recovery, the one on the right remains the same, and their purpose no longer matches.

> So: The two partners find a new way to connect, which means the non-recovering partner has to adjust to this "new" person. Or:

> The two partners separate because they no longer have the connection that has kept them together, and they cannot find a new one. Or:

The recovering partner relapses and rejoins the partner as before, thus losing progress and recovery.

It is not necessarily a "bad" thing that these two people can no longer function as a unit. Their connection may have become destructive rather than constructive, though. If their initial joining together was based on something unhealthy for either or both of them, then parting actually allows each to achieve his/her potential without having to adapt to something that is no longer a good fit.

I look at relationships as a kind of "liquid puzzle." Each partner moves, changes, adapts to the other within the framework of their relationship. As one changes or moves, so must the other if the relationship is to be maintained. See **Recovery.**

Reinforcement: *responses to behaviors that encourage those behaviors to be repeated.*

Paying Blossom for her work reinforces her behavior of doing her job properly. Laughing at Blossom when she gets drunk reinforces her getting drunk. Reinforcement can be a positive experience, but it can also be a function of enabling, such as continuing to make excuses for someone else. See **Enabling.**

Relapse: *picking up the addiction once again after a period of sobriety.*

It is said that "relapse is a part of recovery." This is an extremely dangerous idea, not because relapse doesn't occur – it does. It's because if I as a counselor tell my clients this, they may leave with the idea that it's OKAY to relapse, that they can go ahead and have another drink/toke/poke/whatever. The fact is, your next relapse might kill you or someone else. I don't speak of relapse without making certain that my clients discuss and fully understand this idea. Relapse happens, it's dangerous, and it often results in people thinking, "Well, I've used again, so I may as well *good* and use." It's definitely a shame monster, and when it happens, it needs to be accepted with compassion and understanding. See **Setting Yourself Up, Slip, Falling Off the Wagon.**

Relationships: *the dance between two or more people in regular communication.*

Communication can be seen as the exchange of information by mutually-understood terms. When the terms used by one person change, if the others don't adapt, the communication is no longer possible. So when a person in a relationship changes, if the relationship is to continue, there must be adaptation on each side. Why not call it a dance?

Religion: (*here we go!*) *a belief system that a person thinks is necessary to existence.*

"Religion is for people afraid to go to hell; spirituality is for people who've *been* there." Some who are skeptical of the 12-Step programs say they don't like them because they are *religious*, because they mention God. In truth, these programs speak of *God as we see him/her*. The belief in a Higher Power of some sort is necessary for the rounding-out of a recovery program, to underscore the idea that recovery is not possible without help. Finding comfort with the terminology might be difficult; but it's a really great excuse to keep doing things that clearly don't work.

In my decades of substance abuse counseling, religion is the number one switched addiction, the first choice of many who enter recovery. It makes sense: since my drug no longer gives me that immediate gratification, perhaps God will. ANNNH (that's the sound of the buzzer signifying an incorrect answer – I can't figure out how else to spell it) (Is that why *onomatopoeia* is so difficult to spell?)(I got *that* right the first try). God/the Goddess/Whomever will not do anything for those unwilling to help themselves, thus sitting and waiting around for a Higher Power to end one's addiction is an exercise in the highest level of futilities.

This is not to say that religion is a bad thing, or that it isn't genuine. But it's wise to pay attention and make sure that such conversions *are* genuine and not simply replacement of the chemical.

Religion comes from outside of a person. Many may be insulted by this statement, but the ability of any person to change from one religion to another proves the point, and it's not meant to be a criticism. One's spirituality guides the choice of religion (to either go to a new one or to stay with the one you were born with). *See* **Spirituality, Higher Power.**

Repression: *a defense mechanism by which one can "forget" things from one's consciousness in order to avoid the pain of realization.*

I have two large scars on my left arm. When I was very little, I reached up to the table and spilled my mother's just-poured and scalding coffee onto my arm. I was wearing a wool shirt, and when it was removed, the skin of my arm went with it. I have absolutely no memory of this, not only of the incident itself, but the time it took to heal. As far as I'm concerned, I have *always* had these scars. This is repression.

Resentment: *a naturally-occurring roadblock to recovery.*

Nelson Mandela said, and I don't pretend to be exact in my quoting: "Having resentment against someone is like drinking poison and thinking it will kill your enemy." Carrying a resentment brings weight to the carrier while not affecting its object at all. The sooner one can release resentments – a difficult task indeed! – the sooner one can progress.

Resistance: *Step One in how to avoid getting into recovery.*

Resistance takes many forms, almost too many to mention. Denial is certainly a major form, but there's also compliance, rationalization, projection, blaming, minimizing, maximizing; in short, anything that takes the responsibility from the addict and places it *any*where else. Not the least of these is deciding that one's counselor is an ignoramus.

~ S ~

Schedule Drugs: *Drugs are organized (scheduled) into groups based on their risk of abuse or harm.*

Schedule does NOT refer to the time(s) you must get high every day.

Schedule I drugs have no currently accepted medical use in the US, a lack of accepted safety for use under medical supervision, and a high potential for abuse. Examples: heroin, LSD, marijuana (though this may be changing due to its growing acceptance medically), peyote, meth, and Ecstasy.

Schedule II drugs have a high potential for abuse which may lead to severe psychological or physical dependence. They include: Dilaudid®, methadone, meperidine, oxycodone, methamphetamine, morphine, and others.

Schedule III drugs have less potential for abuse than those in Schedules I and III, with moderate to low physical dependence or high psychological dependence. Examples: products containing less than 15 mg of hydrocodone per dosage unit (Vicodin®), codeine (not more than 90 mg per dosage unit), and buprenorphine (Suboxone®), anabolic steroids, and others.

Schedule IV drugs have a potential for abuse lower still: Xanax®, Soma®, Valium, Halcion®, and others.

Schedule V drugs have a lower potential still than the others and consist primarily of preparations containing limited quantities of certain narcotics, such as cough preparations containing less than 200 mg of codeine per 100 ml, like Robitussin AC® and others. See **APPENDIX 3.**

Self-awareness: *a perhaps overused term to explain the increase in self-knowledge when we begin to fully explore and address characteristics of our lives.*

The more this can occur, the better are our chances of developing a good recovery program. This means not only coming to grips with our personal challenges, but also becoming aware of our strengths and positive qualities. I was a very good softball pitcher (slow-pitch, 12-ft. arc) up through my fifties (one perfect game on my record, though that was clearly a team effort – had I been out there all alone, I'd still be trying to get out of the first inning). Despite my prowess on the mound, I would not trust myself to fix my own or anyone else's computer, or automobile. No problem either way; the self-awareness simply allows for me to do what I do well, to work on those things I hope to improve, and completely leave alone those things impossible or totally uninteresting to me. My own recovery is one of the things I work constantly on.

Self-Help: *a potentially dangerous term, in that it suggests that we can fix all our problems by ourselves.*

Let's face it – if you read a book about, say, improving your memory, is that self-help? Someone else has compiled all the information, written the book, and gotten it published. Granted, you picked the book up, all by yourself, but where would you be without the information that was waiting for you? It's a good term, self-help, but the positivity of it lies in the willingness of the individual to do the work in the first place. The self-help section of your local library is a misnomer, isn't it, really? If it were truly self-help, then that section of the library would be empty. *Self-help* refers to the willingness to use other people's information to get yourself well.

Perhaps *self-work* would be a more appropriate term. The positive part of this all, though, without my being so picky, is that we're willing to address issues in our lives and strive to make changes for the positive. It also shows a willingness to accept the help in some form; from there it can be easy to receive it from other people. Even AA's Big Book is full of the experiences of others, showing our interdependence on one another.

Serenity: *the peace that comes with self-knowledge, self-respect, and self-acceptance.*

Serenity *is* peace. It is calm. It is *grace*. It's being here now. It's mindfulness. It's the realization that, at any moment in time, I have what I need to make it through that moment.

I used to believe that I wanted serenity all the time. Then I realized that I don't necessarily want to be serene when I'm pitching a softball game, or making a serious point for a client or group, or any other number of times. What is comforting for me, though, is the realization that I can call on my serenity at any time. It has sustained me through twenty years of recovery, and I expect it will sustain me through my work for the rest of my life.

Setpoint: *that which is "normal" in a person's body or way of thinking (perhaps).*

For example, a common setpoint, or norm, for temperature in most people is 98.7. Our blood pressure, on the other hand, will differ from person to person. In this, we each have our own setpoint. Setpoints can change. Our response to alcohol, for example, will change the more we drink, raising our setpoint and increasing *tolerance*. See **Tolerance, Addiction, Stress.**

Setting Yourself Up: *overconfidence in recovery.*

A step toward relapse. People often believe they've "got this down," that they're in enough control that "just one little drink won't hurt." Hanging around other users, places, and things can result in an attack on the recovery defense mechanism. There are as many ways to set yourself up as grains of sand on the beach.

Shame: *the third leg of the foundation of* **Rage***; our own negative self-judgment after we have done something inappropriate to another; a lie told to diminish the worth of someone/ourselves.*

Addiction is often said to be a disease of shame. I agree. The loss of self-esteem (if it was ever there in the first place), the feeling of being less-than, inherited from those who, when we were children, taught us that we weren't worthy. Worthy of what? Respect, protection, justice, a voice with which to speak out, education in appropriate coping skills, etc. A parent says to a child, "You ruined my day!" Really? Who, then, is in charge? Do children really have that power? This not only is the birth of carried shame (sometimes for lifetimes), but also teaches the child that he has more power than he really has, and is thus the birth of grandiose thinking. "I can do this to Mom and Dad!" Bad idea.

Shame is a lie. It tells us things that are not true. We slip on the ice, or we trip over something that isn't really there ("Who waxed this lawn?). These things happen to the best of athletes, but it doesn't make us clumsy. Perhaps we're sometimes victims of gravity surges, or our tongues get tied up, or we forget things. Holy Cow! Our humanity is showing! *See* **Emotions, Anger, Fear.**

Should: *a Shame word that puts unnecessary pressure on us.*

"I *should* have known better." "I shouldn't have done that." These are expressions of inadequacy, telling us that we are less than we *should* have been. Toward what end? It's hard to hear the word without thinking we didn't do it correctly, when we were, in fact, doing the best we could at that particular moment, given all circumstances (including those of which we are unaware). I have done my best to eliminate the word from my vocabulary; failing that, I'm aware of every time I use it, and I try to restate any thought in which it occurred. I don't say, "I shouldn't have said *should*."

Slip: *a term for indulging in one's addiction during recovery, usually for a short time.*

The term "slip" is used incorrectly, as it implies an accident. People slip on the ice. They rarely slip onto a bottle of beer, or stumble into a needle, or fall into line of coke. The term I prefer to use is ***skip***, as in, "I skipped a step in my recovery process." *Skip* signifies the acceptance our accountability for the decision to pick up again. Most of my clients, at least the serious ones, readily accept this terminology. *See* **Falling Off the Wagon.**

Slippery Slope: *the approach to any area that is risky for a recovering addict or alcoholic.*

When we start believing that we may have this licked, or that we can learn to drink or use safely, we are on the slippery slope. Any such thinking represents great danger to the recovering person. There are professionals who believe, for example, that alcoholics can learn to drink safely. Others think that, if that's so, then the person wasn't alcoholic to begin with. At any rate, it's an extremely dangerous idea to present to a client – after all, the counselor who believes this is not at risk, right? I had a client who was close to the end of the necessary counseling regimen to regain his driving license. His counselor had espoused the safe-drinking idea, so a week before completion, the client drank, receiving another driving under the influence arrest. His actions were certainly his fault, but some responsibility lies with the counselor *in whom the client trusted* for, basically, encouraging the man to try it again. If drinking has caused problems in the past, how can a counselor justify such encouragement? In this particular case, the client wrote to the agency after his arrest and told them about this counselor's beliefs. The counselor was immediately fired.

Snakes, Recognizing: simply, *awareness.*

This story: A man found a snake in the snow. Being a kind man, he took the snake in. He kept it warm during the winter in a box near the fire, and he fed it for the duration of the freezing weather. Spring came, and the man reached into the box to get the snake so he could release it. The snake bit him. Amazed, the man asked, "Why did you bite me? I took you out of the cold, fed you and sheltered you, and without me you would have died." The snake replied, *"You knew I was a snake when you brought me in."*

This allegory relates to the need to know what those around us may do. It explains why most people don't remarry people they've divorced. More importantly, it brings to us the awareness of our own part in what happens to us. *Fool me once – your fault. Fool me twice – my fault. Fool me three times*

— *addiction.* It's hard for people to get the point, though. One client told me that his first OUI was because he was on the highway, so he took a back road and got his second OUI – this time because his tail-light was out. When he got his third OUI, he decided it might be because he was drunk. Go figure. *See* **Trust, Boundaries, Steve.**

Sober: *the state not only of abstinence, but also working a conscious program to address the problems behind one's drug or alcohol use.*

People who are sober usually become so through a lot of work. Someone who is dry can put his drink down and strut around showing everyone how easy it was for him to do so. Someone sober, on the other hand, remembers how difficult it was to become so, and carries with him the fear of relapse – enough fear for him to be aware, constantly vigilant, and paying attention. People who are dry have something to prove; those who are sober have something to learn. *See* **Dry, Recovery.**

S.O.S.: *Significant Other's Signal. A formula for helping your addicted loved one recognize that he/she may be heading for a relapse.*

Contrary to customary belief, the addict is *not* usually the first person who recognizes the relapse warning signs. Remember, the addict is a person who didn't recognize he was in trouble for some time. It stands to reason he will not recognize his own relapse triggers and signals. The people closest to him tend to be able to see the sign. This is when tact and knowledge is critical to a successful intervention. When I share this process with addictive clients, I suggest it be someone with whom they have an intimate (not sexual – *see* **Intimacy**) relationship, someone who knows his patterns of behavior – but NOT his sponsor. Ideally, the recovering addict will choose his S.O.S. partner.

If you say to your person (let's say it's your hubby), "Dear, I think you're heading toward a relapse," you will undoubtedly be met by defensiveness (people in recovery have told me this themselves, supporting my own experience), particularly if he believes himself to be doing well. This, due to the nature of the disease, may lead to the actual relapse; at the very least, it will usually lead to an argument, one that you won't win.

So it's necessary to have set rules to the engagement. I suggest this. You prepare between you a code phrase, like "I want to talk to you in fifteen minutes." Because you have discussed this process before, he will know what's coming (all of my clients have gone over this procedure). *Take the fifteen minutes!!* Why? So he can use the time to handle the defensiveness, reminding himself that you are risking his anger by telling him this, that you are willing to do so because you love him. He needs this time.

When the fifteen minutes are up, sit facing one another, in open position (no arms crossed, eye-to-eye contact, neutral position). The verbal exchange is as follows: you begin by saying, "I'm worried you might be heading for a relapse." He responds, "What do you *see*?" He doesn't ask *why* you think so – he's looking for your observations as opposed to your judgments.

So you *don't* respond, "Well, you acted like a jerk to me last night." That's a judgment.

You respond with what you've observed, such as: "you raised your voice to me when we were talking about finances last night," or, "you said you'd be home by 10, and you didn't come in until 12," or "you haven't gone to a meeting in two weeks." Whatever it is you've *seen* that rings a bell, that reminds you of other times he's been using, is what you relate to him.

It's crucial that your examples are clear and totally without judgment, and without blame. "You made me sad" is blaming. You go through your list, ending with something like, "...and I'm afraid you're going to start using/drinking/whatever again." Hubby has the opportunity now to ask *only* for clarification. If he doesn't remember one of your examples, he should state so, and get no argument back. If he's doing this right, his not remembering will be true, so let it go.

When he gets all the clarification, his response is simple: "Thank you," and then he leaves and thinks about what he's heard. He does not use this time to explain things, or to make excuses, *even if he has them*. What's important here is your willingness to put yourself in his presence with hard-to-hear information, even harder if he believes his recovery is going well.

Remember that he may, indeed, believe his recovery is going well. He may believe he's got this licked. It's never licked, and you may be the person who helps him avoid going back into the darkness once again. *See* **Judgment, Observation.**

Spirituality: *an inner force, or sense that encourages us toward the positive.*

An inmate with whom I worked defined spirituality as "where your light comes from." I like that very much (this inmate, by the way, convicted of a major crime, made a point of connecting with every staff member who had positively affected him to thank each individually. A rare gift to those who worked with him. Correctional staff do not see this all that often).

My own definition is that spirituality is my relationship with myself, and how that connects me to other people. Spirituality comes from within; religion, from without. The pilots of 911 were *religious*, certainly, but, in my book, they were nowhere near *spiritual*. It's interesting, isn't it, that we have had many religious wars over the centuries; how many *spiritual* wars have we had? *See* **Religion.**

Sponsor: *an experienced, recovering 12-Step member who "rides herd" on a newly (or not) recovering addict/alcoholic.*

Can a sponsor be someone who is not a member of a 12-Step group? That's not up to me to say. The *idea* of a sponsor, though, is someone who has gone through some form of recovery, done the work necessary and experienced the challenge, the pain, of discovery and self-repair. Someone who quit drinking in one day, without support, without fear, will generally not have the experience necessary to help someone else through the process. Sponsors have hard-earned compassion and should also be role-models for those they help along in the process, with stern and fair standards.

Stages of Change Model: *developed in the 1970's by Prochaska and DiClemente, this explains the steps addicts go through to accept recovery and change.*

Addicts find change extremely difficult, largely because they don't want to accept that there's anything wrong. This model explains the process addicts experience before taking the often drastic steps to address not only that their lives have become out of control, but also that the responsibility for change is up to them. This is extremely difficult to do.

- **Pre-contemplation** - In this stage, we do not intend to take action in the foreseeable future (defined as within the next 6 months or more). We are often unaware that our behavior is problematic or produces negative consequences. In this stage we often underestimate the pros of changing behavior and place too much emphasis on the cons of doing so.

- **Contemplation** - In this stage, we intend to start the healthy behavior in the foreseeable future (defined as within the next 6 months). We recognize that our behavior may be problematic, and a more thoughtful and practical consideration of the pros and cons of changing the behavior takes place, with equal emphasis placed on both. Even with this recognition, we may still feel ambivalent toward changing our behavior.

- **Preparation** (Determination) - In this stage, we are ready to take action within the next 30 days. We start to take small steps toward the behavior change and believe it can lead to a healthier life.

- **Action** – Here we have recently changed our behavior (defined as within the last 6 months) and intend to keep moving forward with that behavior change. We may exhibit this by modifying our problem behavior or acquiring new healthy behaviors.

- **Maintenance** - In this stage, we have sustained our change for a while (defined as more than 6 months) and intend to maintain the behavior change going forward. We are now working to prevent relapse to earlier stages.

- **Termination** - *In this stage, we have no desire to return to our unhealthy behaviors and are sure we will not relapse. Since this is rarely reached, and people tend to stay in the maintenance stage, this stage is often not considered in health promotion programs.*

The first time I saw the Termination Stage was when I was doing research for this publication, and its definition explains why. It is extremely dangerous for addicts to believe that they have solved their problems, that their addiction is forever banished. No matter how much work has been done, those inappropriate synapses still exist within their brains and can spring into action without the person knowing that it's coming. Recovery takes ongoing vigilance, self-knowledge, and humility.

I know far too many people who have relapsed after years of successful recovery (although it can be argued, but not by me, that those years weren't "successful" if they ended in relapse. Why be that negative?). It's too easy to believe we've "got it licked," when, in fact, there are probably a couple of synapses just biding their time, waiting for that moment of inattention. Someone very close to me had many years of recovery, then was in an accident. Before too long he realized he was using his pain meds for the wrong reasons, and he went back and got a new chip. All who know him are grateful that he was that aware of how he was doing. See **Synapse.**

Steve: *This is Steve. He is so-named because my wife won't let me give the name to one of our cats.*

When I push Steve's shoulders down toward his feet, after a few seconds, he will backflip. Depending on the surface, he may or may not land on his feet, as you seem him here. However he ultimately lands, though, he will *always* flip. It doesn't matter who performs this action: Steve will always do *the same thing* – FLIP. It's not about me; it's not about you; it's not about who pushes him down. It's totally about Steve. I use this to demonstrate about boundaries.

Once people understand the *Principles of Steve*, one needs only mention his name, and the point is made.

We know certain people will behave in certain ways, just as we know puppies will make messes until they learn other behaviors. Though we might have to *do* something about it, it's not about us. Understanding this helps people realize that they are not governed by the actions of others, but rather have choices as to how to react. See **Boundaries.**

Stimulant: *a chemical that heightens bodily functions (increases neurotransmission levels).*

Legal stimulants include caffeine, nicotine, Ritalin, and others. Their legality does not make them either safe or non-addictive, however, and should be used in moderation.

Illegal stimulants include cocaine, crack, methamphetamine, amphetamine, and the like.

Some people think alcohol is a stimulant due to the extra energy they (*think* they) have when they drink. Actually, the part of the brain that says "I'm tired" has been depressed. Left alone, they'll probably fall asleep.

Trick Question time: Why do doctors prescribe Ritalin, a *stimulant*, for a child who is already over-stimulated? Does it work in reverse for that child?

No. The stimulant wakes up the *control-center* of the brain and allows the child to monitor his behaviors. So if you run out of Ritalin, try caffeine.

Effects of stimulants may include enhanced alertness, awareness, wakefulness, endurance, productivity, motivation, arousal, locomotion, heart rate/blood pressure, and diminished requirement for food and sleep. Also anxiety, mild, chronic depression, hyperactivity, potential heart failure. See **Depressant, APPENDIX 3.**

Stinkin' Thinkin': *Any thoughts that support the return to, or continuation of, addictive or other dysfunctional behaviors.*

"I've been sober for so long, I bet I can handle just one drink." "I can hang out with my old friends and not use with them." "This pain is too much for me to bear without using." "It's okay for me to use to celebrate my winning the lottery/getting a raise/getting married." "You *have* to drink at a wedding." See **Setting Yourself Up.**

Stress: *any challenge to an organism that results in autonomic nervous system reactions.*

People tend to think that all stress is negative. This is not true. Our body responds exactly the same way to positive challenges that it does to negative: adrenaline, breathing changes, sweat, rise in blood pressure and heart rate, etc. Think about suddenly seeing the blue flashing lights behind you on the highway. What happens inside your body? Those changes noted above. Now imagine you matched all the numbers on your lottery ticket. Same physical responses.

Negative stress is known as *dis*tress; positive, *eu*stress. How do we tell the difference? It depends on what we tell ourselves about it. Some people, for instance, might not feel stressful about singing in front of others. Some people might decide that prison can be good for them.

We may also change our minds about stress as time goes along. Some of you may have gone through an unwanted and painful divorce, only to now find yourself with the love of your life. Your view of your divorce – your stressor – has changed, despite its strength while you were going through the divorce proceedings.

Surrender: *the realization that "my way" has not worked, and I must therefore begin to be open to looking at things differently.*

A lovely word, surrender. It is the first step – the acceptance of the power greater than ourselves (which the addiction has proven to be) over which we cannot triumph. *See* **"Yes, Boss" Moment.**

Survivor: *one who has undergone trauma but refuses to be defeated by it.*

There is no denying that bad things happen to us, and that we are not always the cause of the bad things that happen to us. However, if we see ourselves as a *victim* of those bad things, then we are unable to regain the control of our lives. We can say, "Oh, poor me, I was injured and I can't function normally," we remain stuck in that unhealthy place. When we can say, instead, "I have *survived* this injury and will proceed onward the best I can," we regain both our power and the control of our lives that victimhood takes from us. *See* **Victim, Blame, Bu Hu.**

Synapse: *the pathway developed in the brain as a result of repetition of a particular behavior.*

Addicts develop synapses that lead to the ability to use a drug without even thinking about it. We are so full of synapses that we could probably not count them all. I used to toss a very realistic foam rock at my inmate clients, who generally would respond in the expected, defensive way (to the delight of other men in the group). This automatic response overrode the idea that a counselor would actually do something so harmful, so injurious, and so likely to earn a lawsuit. [They took it for granite!]

Perhaps a better example: anyone who drives a car knows that learning to do so probably started out with some difficulty, with extra steps if you learned on a stick. Think of all the things you had to do to get the car going, and keep it going without stalling. *Put the key in; fasten your seat belt; depress the clutch; turn the key; shift into gear; release the clutch while depressing the accelerator;*

and so on. For straight men, this was complicated by the underlying thought, "I'm going to be such a babe-magnet when I learn to do this." All of a sudden, one day, you got into the car, and you could do it without thinking about it. *That* was when the synapse was completely formed, and what began as unnatural had become natural to you.

How strong is a synapse? How many of us have turned on a light that's already on?

If you drive a stick for most of your life, then you suddenly find yourself in an automatic, what happens? Feeling for the clutch, you hit the brake, and your passengers, surprised, briefly hate you and then never let you forget it. [A stick shifter myself, I once drove a State vehicle, automatic, to take an inmate to an interview about two hours away. I was pretty good; I never once hit the brake. Unfortunately, I did search twice for the gearshift, which, of course, wasn't there. His knee was, though.]

⚖

Thoughts: *Ideas, beliefs, etc., often expressed when people think they're talking about feelings.*

"I feel like today is going to be a good day" is actually a thought; there is no expression of any feeling at all in the statement. "I feel like it's going to rain" may be based on your arthritis, but it's still a thought, a summing up of conditions you may actually be feeling. Confusing, huh? Sorry I brought it up. *See* **Feelings, Emotions.**

Tolerance: *a person's ability to function while under the influence of a chemical (or behavior, or person).*

Tolerance changes, maybe even from episode to episode, while BAC will remain static from episode to episode if there are no changes in the time used, amount, and the person's weight. A 250 pound man can drink 6 normal drinks in an hour and have a .07 BAC; his tolerance, on the other hand, may vary.

Let's use alcohol for this. The building of tolerance means that the body becomes more and more used to the presence of alcohol with each increasing use. When someone can "drink you under the table," this is actually not a good thing, because it means that alcohol – a toxic chemical – is becoming "natural" to the body. The liver and other organs alter their natural purpose in order to process the toxic substance. At some point, the body is no longer tolerant of the alcohol, but *dependent* upon it. In fact, withdrawal from alcohol may cause death if it is abruptly taken from the person. This is why every detox has nurses on staff 24/7, with doctors readily available.

In most states, a BAC of .08 will result in a drunk-driving charge. A late-stage active alcoholic will have a BAC of .20 at any given time. What's frightening about this is that you might not realize the level of BAC due to the person's increased tolerance. See **APPENDIX 1, 2.**

Trauma: *a major life event resulting in psychological damage that often affects, negatively, the way that person lives.*

Trauma often teaches us that we *deserve* what we experienced rather than it's being something that has simply happened to us. Children who experience trauma often believe themselves responsible for it, and that they are therefore somehow less than others. This is why addressing trauma in recovery and treatment is so important. As a counselor, I often heard clients say "Why do I have to look at what happened when I was a kid? It wasn't so bad; I got through it, I survived it." True enough – but getting through something doesn't mean that the trip was a healthy one, or that the issues have ever been resolved. A child beaten grows into an angry adult and believes this is the way everyone is raised, justifying his beating of his own children and carrying his anger without even knowing it's there.

It's extremely sad that people minimize what has happened to them; sadder still that they believe themselves either deserving of it or responsible for it. It *happened*. It happened to someone too small and weak to protect himself. See **APPENDIX 3.**

Trigger: *a stimulus that results in an addict using; likewise, any stimulus that results in an action that has become automatic.*

Triggers occur often without our knowing their origin. Adults sometimes have responses to things for which they have no explanation, usually due to some occurrence from childhood that has become buried. Watching the Super Bowl on TV may trigger the desire for beer. Pretending to throw a ball at someone may trigger a defensive response. Most of us can be triggered when we hear a song we relate to a former sweetheart, with positive or negative response.

We have no control over this, and it may come upon us without warning. This is why the recognition of our personal triggers assists in recovery, but it doesn't completely solve the problem. We'll never know all of our triggers; it's important, therefore, to be able to recognize *that* we are being or have been triggered.

Trigger Response: *a response that we give without having to think about it, whether or not it is true or accurate.*

"How are you?" "Fine." Really? People say "fine" when they're having a bad day, when it's raining, when they have bills due.

In the world of recovery, "fine" has been given two meanings, and here I apologize for the language, which, in the world of recovery, is not always appropriate for Mother's ears: **F**ucking-**I**n-**N**eed of-**E**verything, and **F**ucked up-**I**nsecure-**N**eurotic and-**E**motional. "Fine, thanks, and you?"

Trigger Responses can be changed with awareness, with the overcoming of a destructive synapse. I ask clients: "What would you do if someone hit you in the face?" Inevitably, the response is, "I'd hit them back." "So if you're holding your infant niece in your arms and she hits you in the face, you'd hit her back?" They'd say, "Well, you never *said* I was holding a little girl."

Should I have to specify that? When did the automatic response become violent? What about the particular conditions at that moment?

I roomed for two of my high school years with a Harlem Golden Gloves boxing champion who used to love to box with me, tapping me lightly in the face – "Byap, byap, byap." I had not boxed a day in my life, so, despite my being larger than Andre, I was no match for him. One day, however, in my flailing defense, I actually hit him in the face, and I immediately thought, "I'm going to die." Andre, however, rubbing his jaw, said "Nice one. If you ever do that on purpose, you're done." He was not angry, and he recognized my lack of skills. It was a lesson in restraint and compassion that I have never forgot.

Trust: *confidence in an outcome.*

It occurred to me one day as I was running a group for inmates that this paraphrased dictionary definition is fine as far as it goes, but it doesn't really explain anything. My working definition of trust, therefore, is: *the amount of* safety *we have in someone or something.* We jumped off the diving board into the arms of someone we knew would not let us drown, and we'd be safe. We trust others more and more as we learn that the little bits we give them are not betrayed. Granted, things change (anyone with a bitter ex knows this). I trust my nasty ex-fiancée completely – I know exactly what she's capable of doing, thus I will give her absolutely nothing with which to hurt me. I trust a rattlesnake to strike. Others know how to work with them, and that's great. For my part, though, I'll continue to keep my distance. *See* **Snakes, Recognizing.**

~ V ~

Vengeance: *the "making-right" something that was done to ourselves or to another.*

Gentlemen, pay close attention here. We think it the manly and appropriate thing to "take care of" someone who has harmed one of our loved ones, particularly, say, to beat up someone who has molested one of our children. It is a natural response for a man to have. However, let me help you look a little further into the consequences. This example: your daughter is molested by a man. You know who it is, so you go and beat the bejeesus out of him. You get caught. Despite the sympathy the court may have, you have taken the law into your own hands, and you are put behind bars. Your daughter comes to see you, her hero, and she's very sad that she can't hug you or sit on your lap, or talk to you on any given evening, or have you read her bedtime story to you or tuck her in and kiss her goodnight. She's grateful for what you did for her, but at some point she begins to think, "Daddy wouldn't be here if it weren't for me." <u>She begins to blame herself.</u> Your daughter has now been offended against for the *second* time, and *you take yourself* away from her when what she needs more than anything on this earth is to be comforted by you. You instincts were right on target – but the consequences reach further than you might have thought initially. So let the law take care of it; and if that doesn't work, karma will.

Vengeance, basically, is for *ourselves*, not for the victim. We fool ourselves into thinking it's for us. *See* **Victim Guilt, Abuse,** *Sexual*.

Victim: *one who's trauma has become the victor.*

This does not include those incapable of protecting themselves, such as children, the elderly, or those challenged in some way and thus vulnerable. This refers to adults who have experienced trauma and blame the rest of their lives on that occurrence. *See* **Bu Hu, Blame, Survivor.**

Victim Guilt: *the natural (and unfortunate) tendency of victims to blame themselves for what has been perpetrated upon them. See* **Abuse.**

If we have been victimized early in life, say, as children, we lack the abstract reasoning ability to understand that there was something wrong with the perpetrator; we instead tend to think it was our fault, and that we *should* have been able to stop it ourselves, and that we deserved it. We may carry this erroneous belief into adulthood hood, so that when things go right for us, we wait for the other shoe to drop. This is victim guilt. *See the example in* **Vengeance.**

Voice of Addiction: *something all addicts have heard. It's sultry, seductive, inviting, deceiving, consuming, powerful, dangerous, cunning, hypnotic.*

This voice says "Come to me. I will protect you and take care of you. I love you. You *know* me. There is safety only with me. There are no surprises with me. Come and be with me. I will love you forever. You are mine."

- 𝕎 -

Whispered Message: *the universal message that every human being who is living, has ever lived, and will ever live, receives at the moment of birth and continues to be given throughout life. It is extremely simple:* **"Don't do that!"**

Every time this message is ignored, it gets a little louder. At the beginning, it is so quiet it may actually be ignored. However, each time it is repeated, it grows in its volume and severity. Some only need one or a few repetitions; for others, it may not sink in until they are put into jail or prison; for others, it results in illness, injuries, and other losses. The final message is, of course, death.

Why: *why do some people become addicts or alcoholics, while others seem immune?*

There are a number of theories and ideas about the nature of addiction. Do we inherit it? Is it due to our environment? Is it because some people are simply weaker than others? The answer is not clear. Rather than go into the nature of addiction, including the explanation of such chemicals as tetrahydroisoquinalin and tetrahydrocannabinol, as fascinating as they and their processes may be, there is one answer that encompasses all the possibilities. Pay attention here, because this is really important.

People become addicted because they discover this: *If I do this, I will get that.* If I take this, if I do this, if I see this person, then I will receive something that I like. That's the beginning. After a while, the addiction takes control, and the addict no longer receives the pleasure, but instead simply uses to feel normal.

A Native American truism: *First the man takes a drink, then the drink takes a drink, then the drink takes the man.*

Withdrawal: *the process of ending the use of a drug/behavior/person.*

This is a difficult process; it entails giving up something that has become near and dear, and it will be terribly uncomfortable. In the case of withdrawal from both alcohol and benzodiazepines, the withdrawal is potentially fatal. Whatever the degree, it is no fun, and the person in withdrawal needs the support of family and friends. Stopping drinking "cold turkey" is never recommended without medical supervision. Alcohol withdrawal can be fatal, as the brain and central nervous system experience a rebound after being suppressed by alcohol repetitively for an extended period of time. Sudden removal of the central nervous system depressant can be life-threatening.

Withdrawal symptoms from benzodiazepines or abuse drugs like Xanax or Valium, can also be life-threatening. Those in withdrawal from either alcohol or benzos are wise to consult a medical care provider. Sometimes these drugs are referred to as alcohol in pill form.

I know this has been repetitive. In repetition there is learning.

Wounded Healer: *a great many recovery counselors are themselves in recovery, having experienced trauma, addiction, and other events in their earlier lives, thus taking on this term.*

While there are very few adults who lack some form of childhood trauma in some degree, it is way too easy to expect that such counselors are the only ones who can understand. Clients often will say they couldn't deal with a counselor who has not experienced exactly what they have as the understanding would be lacking.

In fact, *no one* has experienced exactly the same thing any other human has experienced. Even siblings don't share exactly the same family: I don't have exactly the same brothers that my brothers have; for one thing, I don't have me as a brother, as they do. Perhaps a dumb example, but it proves the point. A client once said to me, "You just want us to think like you do." I disagreed, telling him, "If you think like I do, you'll want to go home to my wife. Why would I want that?" *See* **Empathy.**

It is said that you cannot step into the same river twice, due to its changing nature. It could also be said that you can't, therefore, step into the same river once…

"Yeah, but….:" *An oft-used beginning of a sentence which precedes one or more reasons proving that asked-for advice is not really wanted after all.*

The Battle Cry of Resistance, "Yeah, but…" is often heard by counselors who have been asked a question by an addict, usually along the lines of "What can I do about…?", or "What do you think about..?" This could easily fall under the category of *Defense Mechanisms*, as it is a great way to hold on to the idea that "nothing anyone else says will make more sense than what I already believe." It shows an unwillingness to listen to alternatives to addictive behavior, and it is often a sign that someone is not quite ready to do the work needed for recovery. *See* **Denial.**

"Yes, Boss" Moment: *the instant we realize that we're arguing a point that cannot be won (fighting a losing battle).*

This idea came about one day as I was trying to convince my boss of the very great idea I had had. He said, quietly, "No." I took a deep breath and started in again, with more conviction. Again, he said, quietly, "No." I took a deeper breath, looked into his eyes, paused a moment, then said, "This is a 'Yes, Boss' moment, isn't it?" He laughed and said, quietly, "Yes." The "Yes, Boss" moment became very common among the men and women with whom I then worked.

I teach it to my clients. There comes a time when we either realize that it's time to give up, to surrender, or face inevitable defeat. I like the term. It's one of the proudest things I'm of. *See* **Surrender.**

APPENDIX 1 – Effects of Alcohol at Different BAC Levels

BAC Level	Effects from Alcohol
0.02 - 0.03 BAC	No loss of coordination, slight euphoria and loss of shyness. Mildly relaxed and maybe a little lightheaded.
0.04 - 0.06 BAC	Feeling of well-being, lower inhibitions, and relaxation. Judgment is slightly impaired. Minor impairment of reasoning and memory, and less cautious. Your behavior can become exaggerated and emotions (ex. happiness or sadness) felt more intensely.
0.07 - 0.09 BAC	Impairment present in everyone. Driving skills such as vision, steering, lane changing and reaction time are impaired along with balance, speech, and hearing. Feelings of Euphoria in some. Self-control and caution are reduced. Riskier behaviors displayed. Judgment, reason and memory suffer. You are likely to believe that you are functioning better than you really are.
	**0.08 BAC is legally impaired and it is illegal to drive at this level.**
0.10 - 0.12 BAC	Significant impairment to motor coordination and loss of good judgment. Speech may be slurred; balance, vision, reaction time and hearing will be impaired. Probably not thinking straight.
0.13 - 0.15 BAC	Very obviously drunk. Severe impairment to judgment, perception, and major motor skills. Very slow reaction time. Blurred vision, loss of balance and slurred speech. Feelings of well-being starting to be replaced by anxiety and restlessness (dysphoria). Vomiting common.
	**At .15 BAC you are 380 times more likely to be in a fatal crash than you are sober.**
0.16 - 0.19 BAC	The drinker has the appearance of a "sloppy drunk." At this point, most drinkers begin to feel incapacitated. Many social drinkers will pass out. Nausea begins to set in and the drinker has difficulty focusing on any object.
	**The average BAC among fatally injured drivers is 0.17, which is also the average BAC nationally for persons arrested for drunk driving.**

0.20 BAC	Out of it. Confused. Dizzy. Requires help to stand or walk. If injured may not feel the pain. Nausea and vomiting. The gag reflex is impaired and you can choke if you do vomit. Blackouts are likely.
0.25 BAC	All mental, physical and sensory functions are severely impaired. Near total loss of motor function control. Increased risk of asphyxiation from choking on vomit and of seriously injuring yourself by falls or other accidents.
0.30 - 0.40 BAC	Extremely life threatening. You have little comprehension of where you are. You may pass out suddenly and be difficult to awaken. Complete unconsciousness. Coma is possible. This is the level of surgical anesthesia (.35) Death may occur (one in every two at 0.40).
Over 0.45 BAC death will occur in most people	

Important Note: An active, late-stage alcoholic will, *at any time,* have and maintain a BAC of .20 or higher, yet may appear sober to those around them. *This is the effect of* tolerance *on them, and to stop cold their drinking could be fatal.* This is why all shelters and detoxes have nurses on the premises 24/7, and doctors on call.

The body (in actual fact the liver) can metabolize only a certain amount of alcohol per hour. No matter how much or how fast alcohol is consumed, the body can only dispose of it at a rate that is generally accepted as being 1 standard drink per hour, or 1 – 1½ oz. of alcohol. Allowing for individual variations in weight, percent body water, percent body fat, and food intake, the amount of alcohol from one standard drink will peak, in the bloodstream, within 30 to 45 minutes.

The rapid consumption of four or five drinks in one or two hours overwhelms the liver with much more alcohol than it can handle. As a result BAC rapidly increases and continues to do so until drinking is stopped or decreased to a rate of less than one drink per hour. Excessively rapid drinking as frequently practiced on campus will invariably lead to dangerously high BAC levels.

Time Needed to Sober Up

Alcohol leaves the body of at a conservative rate of about 0.5 oz. alcohol per hour or .015 percent of blood alcohol content (BAC) per hour. This is an average rate at which the liver can metabolize (burn off) alcohol. The result is that it can take many times longer to sober up than it took to become intoxicated.

Hours to Rid the Body of Alcohol = Peak BAC/.015

Someone with a BAC of .16, or twice the legal driving limit will require over 10 hours to be completely sober and after 5 hours may still not be under the legal driving limit.

Many late night revelers never think about the time it takes to sober up. Driving or performing safety-sensitive duties the morning after can put anyone at risk. If an individual's breath alcohol content is .20 after an evening of heavy drinking at 1:00 AM, they may not be under the legal driving limit of .08 BAC until approximately 9:00AM later that morning. Imagine how long it might take for the individual to be under the US Department of Transportation's BAC limit of .02.

Can you "sober up" someone who is drunk?

As wonderful an idea as this may be, there is no way to remove alcohol from the blood. Cold showers, coffee, and walking someone around may give you an awake, wet, chilly, angry drunk, and it may keep him from passing out, but it will not make him sober.

The statistics listed here around sobering up are no longer true for people with liver damage.

APPENDIX 2 – BAC Levels – How much can you drink without being over the limit?
Estimated and Approximate BAC for Men

MEN AFTER 1 HOUR OF DRINKING

NUMBER OF DRINKS	BODY WEIGHT (lbs)							
	120	140	160	180	200	220	240	260
1	.02	.01	.01	.00	.00	.00	.00	.00
2	.05	.04	.03	.03	.02	.02	.02	.01
3	.08	.07	.06	.05	.04	.04	.03	.03
4	.12	.09	.08	.07	.06	.05	.05	.04
5	.14	.12	.10	.09	.08	.07	.06	.06
6	.17	.15	.13	.11	.10	.09	.08	.07
7	.20	.17	.15	.13	.12	.10	.09	.09
8	.24	.20	.17	.15	.14	.12	.11	.10
9	.27	.23	.20	.17	.15	.14	.13	.12
10	.30	.25	.22	.19	.17	.16	.14	.13

MEN AFTER 3 HOURS OF DRINKING

NUMBER OF DRINKS	BODY WEIGHT (lbs)							
	120	140	160	180	200	220	240	260
1	.00	.00	.00	.00	.00	.00	.00	.00
2	.02	.01	.00	.00	.00	.00	.00	.00
3	.05	.03	.02	.02	.01	.00	.00	.00
4	.08	.06	.05	.04	.03	.02	.02	.01
5	.12	.09	.07	.06	.05	.04	.03	.03
6	.14	.11	.09	.08	.07	.06	.05	.04
7	.17	.14	.12	.10	.08	.07	.06	.05
8	.20	.17	.14	.12	.10	.09	.08	.07
9	.23	.19	.16	.14	.12	.11	.09	.08
10	.27	.22	.19	.16	.14	.12	.11	.10

MEN AFTER 5 HOURS OF DRINKING

NUMBER OF DRINKS	BODY WEIGHT (lbs)							
	120	140	160	180	200	220	240	260
1	.00	.00	.00	.00	.00	.00	.00	.00
2	.00	.00	.00	.00	.00	.00	.00	.00
3	.02	.00	.00	.00	.00	.00	.00	.00
4	.05	.03	.02	.00	.00	.00	.00	.00
5	.08	.06	.04	.03	.02	.01	.00	.00
6	.11	.09	.06	.05	.03	.02	.02	.01
7	.14	.11	.09	.07	.05	.04	.03	.02
8	.17	.14	.11	.09	.07	.06	.05	.04
9	.20	.16	.13	.11	.09	.07	.06	.05
10	.23	.19	.16	.13	.11	.09	.08	.07

Estimated and Approximate BAC for Women*

WOMEN AFTER 1 HOUR OF DRINKING
BODY WEIGHT (lbs)

Number of Drinks	90	100	120	140	160	180	200	220
1	.03	.03	.02	.02	.01	.01	.01	.01
2	.08	.08	.06	.05	.04	.04	.03	.03
3	.13	.12	.10	.08	.07	.06	.05	.05
4	.18	.17	.14	.11	.10	.09	.08	.07
5	.23	.21	.17	.15	.13	.11	.10	.09
6	.28	.26	.21	.18	.15	.14	.12	.11
7	.33	.30	.25	.21	.18	.16	.14	.13
8	.38	.35	.29	.24	.21	.19	.17	.15
9	.43	.39	.32	.27	.24	.21	.19	.17
10	.48	.44	.36	.31	.27	.24	.21	.19

WOMEN AFTER 3 HOURS OF DRINKING
BODY WEIGHT (lbs)

Number of Drinks	90	100	120	140	160	180	200	220
1	.00	.00	.00	.00	.00	.00	.00	.00
2	.05	.04	.03	.02	.01	.00	.00	.00
3	.10	.09	.07	.05	.04	.03	.02	.01
4	.15	.13	.10	.08	.07	.05	.04	.04
5	.20	.18	.14	.11	.09	.08	.07	.06
6	.25	.22	.18	.15	.12	.10	.09	.08
7	.30	.27	.22	.18	.15	.13	.11	.10
8	.35	.31	.25	.21	.18	.15	.13	.12
9	.40	.36	.29	.24	.21	.18	.16	.14
10	.45	.40	.32	.27	.23	.20	.18	.16

WOMEN AFTER 5 HOURS OF DRINKING
BODY WEIGHT (lbs)

Number of Drinks	90	100	120	140	160	180	200	220
1	.00	.00	.00	.00	.00	.00	.00	.00
2	.02	.01	.00	.00	.00	.00	.00	.00
3	.07	.06	.03	.02	.00	.00	.00	.00
4	.12	.10	.07	.05	.03	.02	.01	.00
5	.17	.15	.11	.08	.06	.05	.03	.02
6	.22	.19	.15	.11	.09	.07	.06	.04
7	.27	.24	.18	.15	.12	.10	.08	.06
8	.32	.28	.22	.18	.15	.12	.10	.09
9	.37	.33	.26	.21	.17	.15	.12	.11
10	.42	.37	.30	.24	.20	.17	.15	.13

IMPORTANT NOTE: **BAC and Tolerance are not the same thing**. Your BAC will be exactly the same if you drink the same number of the same types of drinks two nights in a row. However, your *Tolerance* – how you can handle what you drink – might be extremely different. SO USE THESE CHARTS WISELY; YOU DON'T GET TO KEEP DRINKING IF YOUR TOLERANCE IS LOW. If a 240 lb. man with a low tolerance drinks 5 drinks in one hour, he will have a BAC of .06, which is under the legal limit – but he'll probably be very unsafe behind the wheel due to his lower tolerance.

Number of Drinks: What is a drink? As defined under ~ D ~ in Addictionary, a drink is one 12 ounce beer, one glass of wine, one one-shot drink. A Long Island Iced Tea is not one drink, nor is a Velvet Hammer, nor are drinks you're served when you're best friend is the bartender. A drink refers to roughly 1 – 1½ oz. of alcohol in whatever form it arrives to your waiting hand.

[My late father told of a war-time beer he had in, I believe, Nebraska, that had ether in it. Warned not to have more than one, he had more than one and awoke on the floor of the bus on the way back to the base. This would not count as one drink.]

Many people believe these charts to be wrong. Please understand that they are *not* wrong. The fact that you can walk upright after drinking a twelve-pack does not mean that you are sober; it means you have a tolerance to alcohol that allows you to function despite the BAC level. This is tolerance, and the ability to drink a great deal without adverse effect is not something to be proud of, but rather a warning sign that alcohol is finding a home in your body. We might think the ability to drink others "under the table" is a good thing; the reality is that it's damaging the liver and is an extremely dangerous practice.

APPENDIX 3 - Categories & types of drugs, and their effects.

CANNABINOIDS
Marijuana (street names: Blunt, dope, ganja, grass, herb, joint, Mary Jane, pot, reefer, green, sinsemilla, skunk, weed etc.)

Hashish (street names: Boom, gangster, hash, hash oil, hemp, etc.)

Acute Effects: Euphoria; relaxation; slowed reaction time; distorted sensory perception; impaired balance and coordination; increased heart rate and appetite; impaired learning, memory; anxiety; panic attacks; psychosis
Health Risks: Cough, frequent respiratory infections; possible mental health decline; addiction

OPIOIDS (NARCOTICS)
Heroin (street names: Diacetylmorphine, smack, horse, brown sugar, dope, H, junk, skag, skunk, white horse, China white, etc.)

Opium (street names: Laudanum, paregoric: big O, black stuff, block, gum, hop, etc.)

Acute Effects: Euphoria; drowsiness; impaired coordination; dizziness; confusion; nausea; sedation; feeling of heaviness in the body; slowed or arrested breathing
Health Risks: Constipation; endocarditis; hepatitis; HIV; addiction; fatal overdose

Fentanyl: Synthetic opioid similar to morphine (another opioid) but 50 – 100 times more potent.

STIMULANTS
Cocaine (Street names: Cocaine hydrochloride: blow, bump, C, candy, Charlie, coke, crack, flake, rock, snow, toot, etc.)

Amphetamine (Street names: Biphetamine, Dexedrine: bennies, black beauties, crosses, hearts, LA turnaround, speed, truck drivers, uppers, etc.)

Methamphetamine (Street names: Desoxyn: meth, ice, crank, chalk, crystal, fire, glass, go fast, speed, etc.)

APPENDIX 3 - Categories & types of drugs, and their effects, p. 2

Acute Effects: Increased heart rate, blood pressure, body temperature, metabolism; feelings of exhilaration; increased energy, mental alertness; tremors; reduced appetite; irritability; anxiety; panic; paranoia; violent behavior; psychosis, Severe dental problems (for methamphetamine), Nasal damage from snorting (for cocaine)

Health Risks: Weight loss, insomnia; cardiac or cardiovascular complications; stroke; seizures; addiction

DEPRESSANTS

Acute Effects: Depressants slow down activity in the central nervous system of your body. These drugs are also called "downers" because they slow the body down and seem to give feelings of relaxation. Depressants are available as prescription drugs to relieve stress and anger, although drowsiness is often a side effect. The "relaxation" felt from these drugs is not a healthy feeling for the body to experience, to stop abuse of this drug, drug treatment is suggested.

Types of drugs:

- Barbiturates (downers, reds)
- Benzodiazepines (Benzedrine, bennies, peaches, tranquilizers)
    - **Examples:** clonazepam (Klonopin), lorazepam (Ativan), diazepam (Valium) and alprazolam (Xanax)
- Flunitrazepam
- GHB (Gamma-hydroxybutyrate)
- Methaqualone
- Alcohol

CLUB DRUGS

These drugs are often used by young adults at all-night dance parties, dance clubs and bars. They include:
MDMA (methylenedioxy-methamphetamine). Street names: Ecstasy, Adam, clarity, Eve, lover's speed, peace, uppers, etc.

APPENDIX 3 - Categories & types of drugs, and their effects, p. 3

Flunitrazepam (Street names: forget-me pill, Mexican Valium, R2, roach, Roche, roofies, roofinol, rope, rophies, etc.)

GHB (Street names: G, Georgia home boy, grievous bodily harm, liquid ecstasy, soap, scoop, goop, liquid X, etc.)

Acute Effects of Club Drugs

For MDMA - Mild hallucinogenic effects; increased tactile sensitivity; empathic feelings; lowered inhibition; anxiety; chills; sweating; teeth clenching; muscle cramping.

For Flunitrazepam - Sedation; muscle relaxation; confusion; memory loss; dizziness; impaired coordination
For GHB - Drowsiness; nausea; headache; disorientation; loss of coordination; memory loss
Health Risks: for MDMA - Sleep disturbances; depression; impaired memory; hyperthermia; addiction
For GHB - Unconsciousness; seizures; coma

DISSOCIATIVE DRUGS
These include: **Ketamine, PCP and analogs, Salvia divinorum, Dextromethorphan (DXM)**

Acute Effects: Feelings of being separate from one's body and environment; impaired motor function
For Ketamine - Analgesia; impaired memory; delirium; respiratory depression and arrest; death
For PCP and analogs - Analgesia; psychosis; aggression; violence; slurred speech; loss of coordination; hallucinations
For DXM - Euphoria; slurred speech; confusion; dizziness; distorted visual perceptions
Health Risks: Anxiety; tremors; numbness; memory loss; nausea

HALLUCINOGENS
They include **LSD, Mescaline, Psilocybin ('shrooms)**

Acute Effects: Altered states of perception and feeling; hallucinations; nausea
For LSD - Increased body temperature, heart rate, blood pressure; loss of appetite; sweating; sleeplessness; numbness, dizziness, weakness, tremors; impulsive behavior; rapid shifts in emotion

For Mescaline - Increased body temperature, heart rate, blood pressure; loss of appetite; sweating; sleeplessness; numbness, dizziness, weakness, tremors; impulsive behavior; rapid shifts in emotion

APPENDIX 3 - Categories & types of drugs, and their effects, p. 4

For Psilocybin - Nervousness; paranoia; panic
Health Risks: for LSD - Flashbacks, Hallucinogen Persisting Perception Disorder

OTHER COMPOUNDS
Anabolic steroids (Anadrol, Oxandrin, Durabolin, Depo-Testosterone, Equipoise: roids, juice, gym candy, pumpers)
Inhalants (Solvents (paint thinners, gasoline, glues); gases (butane, propane, aerosol propellants, nitrous oxide); nitrites (isoamyl, isobutyl, cyclohexyl): laughing gas, poppers, snappers, whippets

Acute Effects: for Anabolic steroids - No intoxication effects, Also, for Inhalants (varies by chemical) - Stimulation; loss of inhibition; headache; nausea or vomiting; slurred speech; loss of motor coordination; wheezing
Health Risks: for Anabolic steroids - Hypertension; blood clotting and cholesterol changes; liver cysts; hostility and aggression; acne; in adolescents—premature stoppage of growth; in males—prostate cancer, reduced sperm production, shrunken testicles, breast enlargement; in females—menstrual irregularities, development of beard and other masculine characteristics

Also, for Inhalants - Cramps; muscle weakness; depression; memory impairment; damage to cardiovascular and nervous systems; unconsciousness and sudden death.

Important note: Drug are much like computers: things develop very quickly, and they likewise become obsolete (not as quickly) before we're aware. This list, for example, does not include **BATH SALTS** (not to be confused with Epsom Salts), a synthetic drug whose effects include uncontrollable craving for the drug, insomnia, false euphoria rapidly evolving into paranoia, nightmares, depression, severe agitation, hallucinations and delusions, and self-harm.

A drug recently gaining press is **KROKODIL**. The medical name for the drug is desomorphine. It is made at home by acquiring codeine, sold over the counter for headaches, and cooking it with paint thinner, gasoline, hydrochloric acid, iodine and the red phosphorous from matchbox strike pads. Originating in Russia and known as the Zombie Drug, this causes the skin to rot, and life expectancy of users is two to three years at best. There are graphic images online of this drug. It's not pretty. There are rumors of its having made its way to the US, particularly the Mid-West, but these are unconfirmed as far as I know.

APPENDIX 4 – The Effects of Violence on Children.

As with other trauma types, children's responses to domestic violence vary with age and developmental stage. In addition, children's responses depend on the severity of the violence, their proximity to the violent events, and the responses of their caregivers.

The table below shows a brief list of possible reactions/symptoms by age: young children (birth to age 5), school-age children (aged 6 to 11) and adolescents (aged 12 to 18).

The reason this information is included in this publication is that research shows that the majority of addicts (including alcoholics) experienced significant trauma during their childhood years. The accumulation of the following characteristics makes it understandable that, denied not only the nurturing of their caregivers, but also the role-modeling of coping skills, they have almost no choice but to turn to inappropriate chemicals, dysfunctional behaviors, and people who might not have their best interests at heart. They have to find places where they feel warm, welcome, safe, and loved.

Ages 2-4

• Mimic	• Scared	• No trust
• Act out violently	• Bad language	• Stubborn
• Physical injury	• Slow learner	• Sleeping disorder
• Depression		

Ages 5-12

Violent behavior	Unsocial	Smoking
• Low grades	• Unfocused	• ADD/ADHD
• Disrespectful	• Loud	• Defensive/argumentative
• Run away	• Bedwetting	• Selfishness
• Nightmares/bad dreams		

Teen years

- Drugs
- Alcohol
- Sexual behavior
- Police/law trouble
- Gangs
- Depression/suicide
- Fearful/timid
- Pregnancy
- School delinquency
- Impaired learning
- Super-achiever—academic and/or athletic
- Acting out
- Isolation
- Confusion: sexual, religious, emotional

It is important to remember that these symptoms can also be associated with other stressors, traumas, or developmental disturbances, and that they should be considered in the context of the child and family's functioning. It is also important to understand that when the child moves into a different age group, the old symptoms don't simply disappear, but will be carried as the new symptoms are added.

What chance do these children have of a life without serious baggage? Remember – when a child is beaten, he's likely to blame himself (after all, the beater does), and there is little chance for the development of decent self-esteem.

Does this mean that every addict and alcoholic has suffered trauma or experienced abuse? Absolutely not, but research, again, has shown that the majority of addicts have, in fact, experienced childhood trauma. I happen to believe this is so, and I have since I began doing this work.

APPENDIX 5 – The Addicted Family

The Addict	I use alcohol, or drugs, or sex, or food, or religion, or work, or gambling, or nicotine, AND I use people to take care of my feelings. I'm usually filled with shame and I use my addictions to relieve me of the pain, anger, fear, guilt, joy, and loneliness that I don't express.
	My addictions affect my physical being, my spirituality, and my relationships with others.
	I use because I can't NOT use.
The Enabler	I am usually tired. I protect the Addict to the world while I plead and beg the Addict to change. I'm usually busy but very organized—I appear super-responsible. I can't remember when I last had fun or did not worry.
	I have digestive problems, ulcers, headaches, backaches, high blood pressure, heart problems. I'm nervous, irritable, and depressed so I take prescription drugs. I don't exercise and sometimes I drink, smoke, and eat too much.
	I don't have many friends. I sometimes become overly religious. If I were better, maybe my Addict would quit.
	I am angry and addicted to the Addict.
The Hero Typically the first-born child, or fifth.	I always do what is right. I am an over-achiever and over-responsible. I like control—I am compulsive and a manipulator. I am a perfectionist, critical of everyone, and need approval from everyone. I am the peacekeeper and when people get angry or upset I feel responsible.
	It's my job to "make things right," so I don't talk, or trust, or feel. I try to be good but it's never enough so I feel inadequate and guilty and try harder. My values are distorted.
	I am addicted to the family.
The Scapegoat Typically the second-born child, or sixth.	I don't think I am as good as the hero; I can't compete by being good so I withdraw and act out. Negative attention is better than none. I may run away, act out sexually, steal, lie, drink, or use drugs. I tend to be hostile and defiant when I actually feel hurt, angry, and lonely. I feel abandoned and rejected and don't think much of myself.
	I don't really want to be bad but I have difficulty being honest and difficulty having intimate relationships. I have a distorted value system.
	I am addicted to the negativity in the family.

The Lost Child Typically the third-born child, or seventh.	I am a day-dreamer and loner. I can't compete with the Hero or the Scapegoat so I go away. I feel lonely because I don't get support, nurturing, or reassurance. I don't make friends easily and I don't have much experience about how to live in the world. I don't feel close to either of my parents so I may have questions about my sexual role. I feel worthless and deal with life passively. I am prone to illness and accidents. I find relief in fantasy and food. I do not understand intimacy. I am addicted to "escaping" from the family.
The Mascot/Clown Typically the fourth-born child, or eighth.	I bring comic relief to the family. I am super cute and will do anything for attention or a laugh. I am protected by the family—no one tells me the true story. I feel secure and in control when I get attention so I will not be ignored. I am often smaller than my siblings and wiry with tense muscles. I may be hyperactive and on Ritalin. I feel fear most of the time and I cover it with laughter. I am a manipulator and have difficulty focusing on a topic or making a decision. I am prone to suicide. I am addicted to bringing relief to the family through humor.

Please understand that, though the above occurs enough for experts to have noticed it, it's not written in stone. If you were born into a dysfunctional family and were the fourth child, but you feel lost, you don't have to start acting the clown. This information is provided so people can understand why they may fill a certain role in their families. You might have parts of each role. The last thing this is meant to do is cause you consternation because you're not being dysfunctional in the way you're *supposed* to be.

APPENDIX 6 – The Twelve Steps of Alcoholics Anonymous

1. *We admitted we were powerless over alcohol - that our lives had become unmanageable.*
2. *Came to believe that a Power greater than ourselves could restore us to sanity.*
3. *Made a decision to turn our will and our lives over to the care of God as we understood Him.*
4. *Made a searching and fearless moral inventory of ourselves.*
5. *Admitted to God, to ourselves, and to another human being the exact nature of our wrongs.*
6. *Were entirely ready to have God remove all these defects of character.*
7. *Humbly asked Him to remove our shortcomings.*
8. *Made a list of all persons we had harmed, and became willing to make amends to them all.*
9. *Made direct amends to such people wherever possible, except when to do so would injure them or others.*
10. *Continued to take personal inventory and when we were wrong promptly admitted it.*
11. *Sought through prayer and meditation to improve our conscious contact with God as we understood Him, praying only for knowledge of His will for us and the power to carry that out.*
12. *Having had a spiritual awakening as the result of these steps, we tried to carry this message to alcoholics and to practice these principles in all our affairs.*

Other 12-Step programs adapt these steps to their own particular needs, and there are a great many such programs helping addicts all over the world.

Note that 12-Step programs are not considered therapy, though there is no doubt that they are *therapeutic*. What's the difference? Therapy is treatment, while 12-step groups are support. Individual and group counseling are therapies; sports, leisure time, taking a walk, calling a friend – these are therapeutic. 12-Step programs have warnings against crosstalk, which refers to people speaking out of turn, interrupting someone while they are speaking, or giving direct advice to someone in a meeting. A good counselor rarely if ever gives advice, but rather offers views of alternative behaviors. In crosstalk, we are likely to receive advice or criticism.

APPENDIX 6 – The Twelve Steps of Alcoholics Anonymous, p.2

This is not to say that the experience of a recovering addict is not helpful to someone new in recovery; in fact, it is often such experience that helps the most. But the delving into the deeper issues behind the addictions are best left to those educated in such matters.

A comment about AA and other 12-step programs from an outsider. Me. I'm an outsider because I am not an alcoholic, but rather a Social Drinker (some believe this to be a mythological being). Many people are afraid of AA, though they don't realize it as fear. They believe that AA is a *religious* organization. I suppose, for many, it is, and there are some individual groups that certainly are. I don't see myself as a religious person, and when I attend religious functions (including the UCC Church in which I sing in two choirs), I don't say the prayers. As Thomas Paine once said, "My own mind is my own church," and my thoughts are private and my own. It's the same in a 12-step meeting. They may say God, and I keep quiet and honor my own view of my spirituality.

To refuse to go to a relevant 12-step meeting is to deny oneself the absolute *strength* it has to offer: COMMUNITY. There are few places you can go, even in a strange town, city, or country, where you will be greeted by people who are there for exactly the same purpose you are. I went to my son's 5th Anniversary, where he was the speaker, and people who didn't know me greeted me warmly, offered me the fellowship of the community without asking if I was a member.

Caution: there are closed groups. Respect them. I drove inmates to a closed AA meeting in the community and was not allowed to attend the meeting. Initially insulted, I quickly realized that I had no right to expect them to alter their rules because I was chauffeuring alcoholics to their meeting. I spent a delightful 90 minutes by myself, largely because I've learned to enjoy my own company, and I honestly can't remember the last time I was bored (someone said, "there is no bored; there is only boring." I have taken that to heart, and I have not been bored for over twenty years).

Each 12-step group has its own personality. If you don't like the first one, try the second, and so on, and if you don't like religious-sounding talk, translate it into something you can handle, and enjoy the company.

APPENDIX 7 – KARPMAN'S TRIANGLE OR DRAMA SYSTEM

Karpman drama triangle

The Karpman Drama Triangle models the connection between personal responsibility and power in conflicts, and the destructive and shifting roles people play. He defined three roles in the conflict; Persecutor, Rescuer (the one up positions) and Victim (one down position). Karpman placed these three roles on an inverted triangle and referred to them as being the three aspects, or faces of drama.

1. **The Victim:**

The Victim's stance is *"Poor me!"* The Victim feels victimized, oppressed, helpless, hopeless, powerless, ashamed, and seems unable to make decisions, solve problems, take pleasure in life, or achieve insight. The Victim, if not being persecuted, will seek out a Persecutor and also a Rescuer who will save the day but also perpetuate the Victim's negative feelings.

2. **The Rescuer:**

The rescuer's line is "Let me help you." A classic enabler, the Rescuer feels guilty if he/she doesn't go to the rescue. Yet his/her rescuing has negative effects: It keeps the Victim dependent and gives the Victim permission to fail. The rewards derived from this rescue role are that the focus is taken off of the rescuer. When he/she focuses their energy on someone else, it enables them to ignore their own anxiety and issues. This rescue role is also very pivotal because their actual primary interest is really an avoidance of their own problems disguised as concern for the victim's needs.

3. **The Persecutor (sometimes known as the Perpetrator):**

The Persecutor insists, *"It's all your fault."* The Persecutor is controlling, blaming, critical, oppressive, angry, authoritative, rigid, and superior.

APPENDIX 8 – Drugs Used in Opioid Addiction Treatment

"Drugs are used short-term to get people off opioids and long-term to help keep them in recovery," says Michael Weaver, MD, professor in the department of psychiatry and behavioral sciences and medical director of the Center for Neurobehavioral Research on Addictions at the University of Texas Health Science Center at Houston.

"Withdrawal from opiates is not deadly, but it is very uncomfortable. It feels like a really bad flu and lasts about as long. Most people have trouble making it through one day of withdrawal without the help of medication," Dr. Weaver explains. "We use a drug that can substitute for the opiate and then taper it down slowly."

Current drugs used to treat opioid addiction are classified as agonists, partial agonists, and antagonists. Agonist and partial agonists act like opiates but are safer and less addictive. Opioid antagonists block many of the effects of opiates that lead to addiction. Here are the specifics:

- Methadone is a slow-acting opioid agonist that can be used to prevent withdrawal symptoms and for long-term treatment. Methadone, usually given in an adjustable once-a-day dose, can reduce drug cravings during recovery. It may have some of the same side effects as heroin and can cause depressed breathing in large doses. "One of the main drawbacks to methadone is that it can only be dispensed at a methadone clinic. You need to show up every day to get it," Weaver says. Methadone is a prescription drug for severe pain. As an opiate, methadone is also highly addictive. Opiate addiction leads many patients to find illegal ways to get methadone — even when their prescriptions have expired.
    Long-term use and abuse of methadone can lead to serious health complications. Once you're addicted to this drug, you'll experience painful withdrawal symptoms as you stop taking it. Overcoming methadone withdrawal is tough. But you can quit successfully with the help of your doctor and support from your loved ones. *
- Buprenorphine (Suboxone) is a partial opioid agonist given as an adjustable-dose tablet. It's similar to methadone, but has fewer opioid effects. It may still cause nausea and constipation, but is less likely to cause respiratory depression. "Buprenorphine is less restricted. It can be dispensed at a doctor's office. It is also more expensive, which may be a drawback for some people," Weaver says.

APPENDIX 8 – Drugs Used in Opioid Addiction Treatment, p. 2

- **Naltrexone** is an opioid antagonist. It does not have the effects of an opioid drug and is used only for recovery. "If you try to take an opiate while in recovery, naltrexone will block the high. One drawback is that if you need an opiate drug for pain, it will also block pain relief. You can override the effects of the block with larger doses of opiate, but it is tricky. Buprenorphine can be given as a pill or as a monthly injection," Weaver says. Naltrexone is prescribed less often because people do not tend to stay on it long-term.

Researchers are working on ways to make drug-assisted opioid treatment more effective. A longer-acting version of buprenorphine is being tested. It is given as an implant inserted under the skin that will help maintain recovery for six months.

* Former clients who used methadone report that withdrawal from it is terrible. Also, a friend who was prescribed it for non-addiction issues and in very small doses was visibly extremely uncomfortable when he stopped using it. There are other choices, and using *any* of these products should be done only after getting all the facts and information possible.

It should be noted that drug-assisted treatment is controversial and not for everybody.

WHAT IS VIVITROL® (naltrexone for extended-release injectable suspension)?

VIVITROL is a prescription injectable medicine used to:

- Treat alcohol dependence. You should stop drinking before starting VIVITROL.
- Prevent relapse to opioid dependence **after** opioid detox. You must stop taking opioids or other opioid-containing medications before starting VIVITROL.

VIVITROL must be used with other alcohol or drug recovery programs such as counseling.

VIVITROL may not work for everyone and has not been studied in children.

APPENDIX 8 – Drugs Used in Opioid Addiction Treatment, p. 3

DO NOT TAKE VIVITROL IF YOU:

- Are still using or still have any symptoms of physical withdrawal due to dependence on opioid street drugs or opioid-containing medicines.
- Have opioid withdrawal symptoms.
- Are allergic to naltrexone or any of the ingredients in VIVITROL or the liquid used to mix VIVITROL.

WHAT IS THE MOST IMPORTANT INFORMATION I SHOULD KNOW ABOUT VIVITROL?

VIVITROL CAN CAUSE SERIOUS SIDE EFFECTS, INCLUDING:

RISK OF OPIOID OVERDOSE

Using opioids, even in amounts that you used before VIVITROL treatment, can lead to accidental overdose, serious injury, coma, or death. To avoid accidental overdose:

- **Do not** take large amounts of opioids or try to overcome the opioid-blocking effects of VIVITROL.
- Do not use opioids in amounts that you used before VIVITROL treatment. You may even be more sensitive to **lower** amounts of opioids:
    - After detox
    - When your next VIVITROL dose is due.
    - If you miss a dose of VIVITROL.
    - After you stop VIVITROL treatment.

Get emergency medical help right away if you have trouble breathing; become very drowsy with slowed breathing; have slow, shallow breathing; feel faint, dizzy, confused; or have other unusual symptoms.

SEVERE REACTIONS AT THE INJECTION SITE

VIVITROL may cause severe injection site reactions, including tissue death. Some injection site reactions have required surgery. Call your doctor right away if you notice any of the following at your injection site:

APPENDIX 8 – Drugs Used in Opioid Addiction Treatment, p. 4

- Intense pain
- The area feels hard
- Swelling
- Lumps
- Blisters
- An open wound
- A dark scab

Tell your doctor about any injection site reaction that concerns you, gets worse over time or does not get better by two weeks after the injection.

SUDDEN OPIOID WITHDRAWAL

To avoid sudden opioid withdrawal, you must stop taking any opioids or opioid-containing medications, including buprenorphine or methadone, **for at least 7 to 14 days** before starting VIVITROL. If your doctor decides that you don't need to complete detox first, he or she may give you VIVITROL in a medical facility that can treat sudden opioid withdrawal.

Sudden opioid withdrawal can be severe and may require hospitalization.

LIVER DAMAGE OR HEPATITIS

Naltrexone, the active ingredient in VIVITROL, can cause liver damage or hepatitis. Tell your doctor if you have any of the following symptoms of liver problems during VIVITROL treatment:

- Stomach area pain lasting more than a few days
- Yellowing of the whites of your eyes
- Dark urine
- Tiredness

VIVITROL can cause other serious side effects, such as:

- **Depressed mood** – Sometimes this leads to suicide or suicidal thoughts and behavior. Tell those closest to you that you are taking VIVITROL. You or those closest to you should call your doctor right away if you become depressed or have any new or worsening depression symptoms.
- **Allergic pneumonia** – Tell your healthcare provider if you have shortness of breath, wheezing, or a cough that doesn't go away.

Serious allergic reactions – Get medical help immediately if you have a skin rash; swelling of your face, eyes, mouth, or tongue; trouble breathing or wheezing; chest pain; or are feeling dizzy or faint.

Vivitrol is extremely expensive in this country; it is less so in Canada.

[**NOTE:** Since the volume was begun, there has been some use of Vivitrol within the jails in Maine, and it appears to be affective at this point. Law Enforcement officials note that a major problem within jails is inmates who come in while being in a medically-assisted recovery program, using Suboxone or Methadone. Vivitrol can help with these inmates who would otherwise end up with withdrawal.]

APPENDIX 9 – Johari's Window

Understanding the Johari Window model

A Johari window is a psychological tool created by Joseph Luft and Harry Ingham in 1955. It's a simple and useful tool for understanding and training:

- self-awareness
- personal development
- improving communications
- interpersonal relationships
- group dynamics
- team development; and
- inter group relationships

It is one of the few tools out there that has an emphasis on "soft skills" such as behaviour, empathy, co-operation, inter group development and interpersonal development. It's a great model to use because of its simplicity and also because it can be applied in a variety of situations and environments.

In this example we are going to talk about how the Johari window works with an individual within a team. In this instance there are two factors at work within the Johari window. The first factor is what you know about yourself. The second factor relates to what other people know about you.

The model works using four area quadrants. Anything you know about yourself and are willing to share is part of your open area. Individuals can build trust between themselves by disclosing information to others and learning about others from the information they in turn disclose about themselves.

Any aspect that you do not know about yourself, but others within the group have become aware of, is in your blind area. With the help of feedback from others you can become aware of some of your positive and negative traits as perceived by others and overcome some of the personal issues that may be inhibiting your personal or group dynamics within the team.

W

APPENDIX 9 – Johari's Window, p.2

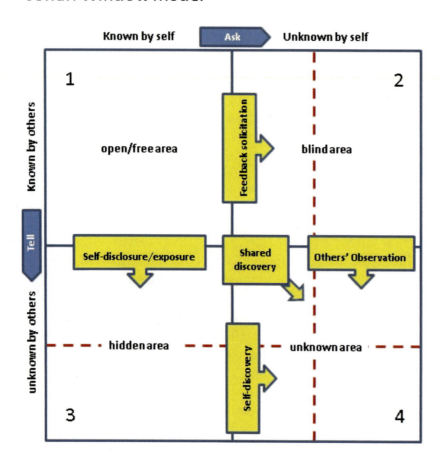

There are also aspects about yourself that you are aware of but might not want others to know, this quadrant is known as your hidden area. This leaves just one area and is the area that is unknown to you or anyone else – the unknown area.

APPENDIX 9 – Johari's Window, p.3

The balance between the four quadrants can change. You might want to tell someone an aspect of your life that you had previously kept hidden. For example, maybe you are not comfortable contributing ideas in large groups. This would increase your open area and decrease your hidden area.

It is also possible to increase your open area by asking for feedback from people. When feedback is given honestly to you it can reduce the size of your blind area. Maybe you interrupt people before they have finished making their point which can cause frustration. Alternatively people may always want to talk to you because you are a good listener. Sometimes you don't realise these aspects of your character until it is pointed out.

By working with others it is possible for you to discover aspects that neither of you may never have appreciated before.

Some examples of unknown factors can be as follows:

- an ability that is under-estimated or un-tried through lack of opportunity, encouragement, confidence or training
- a natural ability or aptitude that a person doesn't realise they possess
- a fear or aversion that a person does not know they have
- an unknown illness
- repressed or subconscious feeling
- conditioned behaviour or attitudes from childhood
- For example in an educational setting, a student's contact with a tutor may help him understand how his experiences both in and outside of school can have an impact on his learning. This discovery about himself would reduce the size of his unknown area.

From a practical point of view in implementing the Johari window you need to look at two steps.

Step one: The place to start in the Johari window is in the open area. Make some notes about yourself. Complete the <u>Self Awareness Diagnostic</u>. What are your strengths and your weaknesses? What are you comfortable with and willing to share with others? Try and be honest and clear about what you know about yourself already.

APPENDIX 9 – Johari's Window, p. 4

Step two: Involve other people and ask for feedback about yourself. Be prepared to seriously consider it. That doesn't mean that you have to do everything that's suggested, but you should at least listen and think about it. Then give the person who provided the feedback some acknowledgement or thanks for making the effort. Depending on how confident you are you might prefer to do this as either a group exercise or on a one to one basis. Remember that giving effective feedback is a skill and some people may be better at it than others. When receiving feedback, be respectful, listen and reflect on what has been said. It may be on receiving feedback you may want to explore it further that can lead to discovery about yourself.

The Johari window as a tool does have its drawbacks:

- Some things are perhaps better not communicated with others.
- People may pass on the information they received further than you desire or use it in a negative way.
- Some people or cultures have a very open and accepting approach to feedback and some do not. People can take personal feedback offensively so it's important when facilitating to exercise caution and start gradually.

There are many ways to use the Johari model in learning and development. It very much depends on what you want to achieve in your training or development activities? What are your intended outputs and how will you measure that they have been achieved? How can the Johari Window theory and principles are used to assist this.

Johari is a very elegant and potent model, and as with other powerful ideas, simply helping people to understand is the most effective way to optimise the value to people. When people really understand it in their own terms, it empowers them to use the thinking in their own way, and to incorporate the underlying principles into their future thinking and behaviour.

The Self Awareness Diagnostic is a great accompaniment to the Johari window model. It helps people to explore the qualities that make them who they are. The simple online questionnaire provides instant feedback to the participant that they can positively use in understanding their personal strengths and weaknesses, what belongs in their open space. It can also objectively help the participant to start to process some of those attributes that reside in their blind spot and can encourage discussion amongst the group without being confrontational or causing contention.

APPENDIX 9 – Johari's Window, p. 5

What is unique about the Self Awareness Diagnostic is it explores not only an individual's 'soft skills' and working style preferences but also how participants like to learn; their learning styles. In an education or business environment this can be a great enabler for a teacher or trainer to ensure all the members of the group are motivated and able to achieve their full potential.

Clarification: Before treatment, most people can be represented by the upper left hand quadrant of the diagram, designated in blue ink. The goal of treatment is to reach the upper left quadrant designated by the dotted red line.

Quadrant 1: That which is obvious. "I'm tall, bearded, and I have blue eyes." Things everyone can see about us: the clothes we are wearing, and so on.

Quadrant 2: That which we cannot see but others may be able to. Has anyone ever said you sound angry, but you didn't realize it?

Quadrant 3: That which is hidden. "I have a secret, and I'm not going to tell you." In therapy, we can unburden ourselves of some of these items. This is AA Step 5.

Quadrant 4: The unknown, as in, "I don't know why I am so afraid of spiders." We might be able to discover why we sometimes act as we do, particularly when our responses come from things from our past.

During treatment, we learn more about Quadrants 2, 3, and 4, both by being told things and by asking for information.

APPENDIX 10 – Myths and Addendums (in other words, items I forgot)

Geographical Cure: *If I move, I can put a stop to my addiction.*

We are told that moving will not produce recovery. This is true, in essence. However, when we're on the recovery path, it makes sense not to frequent places in which we've used, or hang out with the people with whom we've used. Moving, by itself, will not work; after all, if you pack a jerk, you unpack a jerk (a nicer word than used in the original). This suggestion is made in the same spirit in which we recommend that recovering alcoholics don't become bartenders or live above bars.

Perfection: *a goal impossible to attain in recovery.*

Recovering addicts often have a belief that they must do recovery perfectly. This comes in part from the immediate gratification ("I want it, I want it all, and I want it NOW!"). They've learned all this new stuff, whether from counselors, 12-steppers, or whomever, and they want to do it as well as "everyone else." I hate to be the bearer of bad news, but that's not going to happen. Mistakes will be made.

When I got out of rehab, I was reminded not to make any major changes for at least a year, and particularly not to begin any new relationships. I left rehab on November 21, and on the 22nd I met up with my high school art teacher (with whom I'd been in contact throughout the five weeks of rehab – I had run into her brother on the way there, and he gave me her address. I had not seen her for 30 years). Less than a year later, we were married. It was the best decision I've ever made, and 21 years later (at this writing) the honeymoon has yet to end. But for a great many months, I was afraid to get in touch with counselors at my rehab because I thought I was doing it wrong.

There are no hard and fast rules to recovery, and no two recovery pathways are exactly the same. I was given good advice, and I realize now, as I did then, that I was taking a chance. But I also recognized the soul connection and acted on it. Do I recommend others do the same? I neither do nor don't. I only suggest keeping one's eyes open and being careful, and once you know your heart, perhaps it might be wise to follow it.

APPENDIX 10 – Myths and Addendum (in other words, items I forgot), p.2

What I do know is that it took a while for what I learned in rehab to sink in – to make the journey from my head to my heart. That made for some difficulty in the beginning of my relationship with my wife, but as we both were no strangers to self-work, we have built a strong and powerful relationship. Those who questioned me at the beginning are now firm supporters.

Victim Guilt Addendum:

I recently watched two powerful episodes of the excellent TV reality program, *Intervention*. In each, the female addict had been molested as a child, and the second was raped during the filming of her episode. In one case the mother didn't believe her daughter when the rape occurred, and she blamed her fifteen-year-old child for being *provocative* with her (the mother's) boyfriend, with whom Mom immediately moved across the country.

It cannot be stressed strongly enough how often such trauma, and such lack of support, damages a child. In the case above, the father didn't do anything, believing the mother would "take care of it." The result? A vulnerable young girl whose life has been turned upside down, who has not only been violated, but also abandoned by the two people who are supposed to be taking care of her.

My problem with watching *Intervention* is wanting so many times to leap through the screen and throttle some of the parents. If you're going to have children, then understand **that you are responsible for their well-being and safety**, and for their comfort when either is threatened or harmed, until they become adults. It is your job to believe them when they talk about such things, and to realize that no matter how provocatively your daughter may dress, when an adult touches her, IT IS NOT HER FAULT. *Some*one has to be the adult. Through my years of teaching and counseling, I have yet to meet a teenager who is ready to handle adulthood, at least not before the nasty happens. Get it?

Wow. See **Anger**.

Alcohol and/or Drugs are the Problem: *Myth. Alcohol and/or drugs are the **solution** to the problem.*

People believe that drugs and alcohol are the problem with these people who cause everyone such headaches. Would that it were that simple. In fact, they are the solution to problems that the people come up with when nothing else seems to work. In the examples in the Victim Guilt Addendum, with

APPENDIX 10 – Myths and Addendum (in other words, items I forgot), p.3

the two daughters who had lost so much, why *shouldn't* they resort to something that dulls the pain, that becomes a place of welcome and peace? If their support systems fail them, where else can they turn? IT'S NOT THEIR FAULT!

That being said, it *does* become their responsibility. This is not fair, necessarily, but for those who think that it's easy to stop ("Just say NO!), or that addicts are weak, or bad people, it's not that simple. Addiction is a disease, plain and simple.

Extrinsic versus Intrinsic Motivation

Extrinsic motivation is that which comes from outside of us; for example, when parents send their teenager to rehab, or when someone is abstinent because he's on probation and will go back to prison if he uses. Everything *looks* good, but the person knows he's going to use as soon as he's off probation.

Intrinsic motivation, on the other hand, occurs when someone makes the conscious decision *inside* to change. Perhaps she's "sick and tired of being sick and tired," or she's "aged out" of using. Whatever the case, intrinsic motivation is much more powerful than ex, and the chances of successfully entering recovery are vastly improved when the will is one's own.

Needing to Change versus Wanting to Change

Needing to Change: How many of us have said something like, "I need to lose weight?" Usually such a statement comes from Shame, the embarrassment of not being as trim and svelte as we would like. When someone else says to us, "You need to lose weight," we often respond with "Oh, yeah? Who says?" In either case, we generally go about our business without making any change at all. Needing to do something implies some outside force telling us it could be a good idea. On the other hand,

Wanting to Change allows that voice within us to suggest what might be appropriate, and we will listen more easily than we will to that judgmental jerk (which may live within us) telling us what to do.

The bottom line, here, is that *needing* to do something rarely works; *wanting* to do it is much more effective. This is very similar, of course, to *Extrinsic vs. Intrinsic* motivation.

DD

APPENDIX 10 – Myths and Addendum (in other words, items I forgot), p.4

You Can Drink Yourself Sober

This would be hilarious if it weren't so dangerous. I won't suggest trying this, but if you were to have a breathalyzer after trying this, the truth would immediately be evident. This is a factor of **Tolerance**, not of BAC.

APPENDIX 11 – Drug Terms [Note: Terms may change due to many reasons, among them the belief that if the names change, non-users and parents won't catch on

~A~

ACAPULCO GOLD - a very potent strain of marijuana from Acapulco, Mexico.
ACID - LSD (Lysergic Acid Diethlamide)
ACID HEAD - user of LSD, "Acid Freak"
AIR HEAD - under the influence of marijuana
ALCOHOL - booze, juice, sauce
ALLEY JUICE - very cheap wine, "Grapes"
AMPHETAMINES - speed, crystal, crank, meth, black beauties, bennies, uppers, dexies, 357 magnums
ANGEL DUST - Phencyclidine or PCP
ARTILLERY - equipment for shooting drugs

~B~

B's - Heroin
BACK-UP - permitting blood to back up into a syringe to ensure the needle is in a vein
BAD TRIP - unpleasant LSD experience
BAG - packet of drugs, usually a standard amount for sale
BAG MAN - person who transports money
BALLOON - small amount of contained narcotics
BANGING UP - to inject narcotics
BARBS - Barbiturates; "downers, "reds"
BASE - Crack Cocaine
BEAN - capsules for drugs
BEAT - to cheat someone
BENNIES - Benzedrine; "peaches"
BENZOS - Tranquillisers
BID – a prison sentence
BIG C - Cocaine
BIG CHIEF - Mescaline
BIG MAN - supplier of drugs
BINDLE - a small packet of drug powder
BLACK BEAUTIES - Amphetamines
BLACK HOLLIES - Amphetamines
BLACK-OUT - amnesia for events occurring while heavily intoxicated with alcohol, other sedative/hypnotic drugs
BLACK RUSSIAN - Hashish
BLASTED - high on drugs
BLAZE - Marijuana
BLOTTER - LSD
BLOW - smoke Marijuana; sniff Cocaine
BLUE DEVILS - Amobarbital
BLUES - Valium
BLUNTS - a cigar slit open and filled with marijuana
BOMBED OUT - very much intoxicated by narcotics
BOMBITA - mixture of Cocaine & Heroin
BONG - a cylindrical water pipe for smoking narcotics, especially Marijuana
BOOST - to steal
BOOZE - alcohol (beer, wine, liquor)
BREAD - money
BRICK - a kilogram (2.2 pounds) of tightly compacted Marijuana or Hashish
BRING DOWN - come off a drug
BROKER - go-between for a drug deal
BROWN - Heroin
BROWNIES - Ecstasy
BUDS - Marijuana
BUMMER - bad experience with drugs
BUNDLE - multiple bags of a drug

APPENDIX 11 – Drug Terms, p. 2

BURN - cheated by a pusher
BURNOUT - heavy user of drugs
BUSTED - arrested on a drug-related charge
BUTTONS - peyote or mushrooms
BUY - purchase drugs
BUZZED - mildly intoxicated

~C~

C - Cocaine
CANDY - Barbiturates or Cocaine
CANDY MAN - drug supplier
CAPS - drug capsule
CARTWHEELS - Amphetamines
CHARGED UP - under the influence of drugs
CHASING THE DRAGON - a particular way of inhaling Heroin
CHEESE a starter form of Heroin containing Tylenol PM and up to 8 percent heroin
CHARLIE - Cocaine
CHEER - LSD
CHINA WHITE – Methylfentanyl, an opioid analgesic that is an analog of fentanyl
CHIPPING - occasional use of drugs
CHIPPY - person who uses drugs infrequently
CHRISTINA - Crystal Meth
CHRONIC - Marijuana
CLEAN - drug free; not having drugs in one's possession
COASTING - being high on drugs
COCAINE - crack, coke, booth, blow, railers, snow, ringer, divits, toot, cola, rocks, blast, white dust, ivory flakes, nose candy, mobbeles
COKE - Cocaine

COKE BROKE - financially incapacitated from supporting Cocaine habit
COLD TURKEY - sudden withdrawal from drugs
COLOMBO - Marijuana grown in Columbia
COME DOWN - the ending of a drug experience
CONNECT - to purchase drugs
CONNECTION - supplier of drugs
COOKER - usually a spoon or bottle cap used to heat drugs for injection
COP - to obtain drugs
COP-OUT - to evade an issue
CRACK - A pure form of Cocaine usually injected or smoked
CRACK HEAD - someone who is addicted to crack cocaine
CRACK PIPE - A device for smoking crack usually home made
CRASH - to sleep off the effects of drugs
CRYSTALS - Methamphetamine
CUT - to adulterate drugs
CUT OUT - to leave from someplace

~D~

DAGGA - South African word for Marijuana
DARKS - Heroin
DEALER - someone who sells illegal drugs
DECK - a packet of drugs
DEP-TESTOSTERONE - injectable steroid
DEXIES - Dexadrine, or "dex"
DEVIL'S DICK - A pipe, usually for smoking crack
DIAMONDS - amphetamine
DIABLITO - combination of crack cocaine and marijuana in a joint

APPENDIX 11 – Drug Terms, p.3

DIME BAG - $10 worth of a narcotic
DOLLIES - Methadone
DOLPHINS – Ecstasy
DOPE - a general term for drugs of abuse; once used for pot, now refers to heroin.
DOTS - LSD
DOWNERS - Tranquillisers
DRIED OUT - having gone through a withdrawal program for drugs or alcohol
DROP - to take a drugs orally; a place where money or drugs are left
DROP - LSD
DRUGGIE - a narcotic user or addict
DRUNK PILLS - Valium
DUST - narcotics in powder form
DUSTING - sprinkling a narcotic powder on another drug such as PCP on Marijuana
DYNAMITE - high quality, potent drugs

~E~

E's - Ecstasy
EASY SCORE - obtaining drugs without difficulty
EGGS - Tranquillisers
EIGHTH - one-eighth of a pound of drugs
ELEPHANT - PCP
EXPERIENCE - trip on LSD

~F~

FACTORY - place where illicit drugs are prepared for sale
FIX - an injection of drugs
FLAKE -Cocaine
FLASH - LSD
FLASHBACK - recurrence of previous hallucinations
FLEA POWDER - poor quality drugs
FLIP OUT - become psychotic or irrational
FLYING - under the influence of drugs
FOOTBALL - Amphetamine
FREAK OUT - a bad trip; an unexpected reaction to a drug
FREEBASE - smoking Cocaine from a special water pipe
FREEZE - to renege on a drug transaction
FRONT - to put money out before receiving the merchandise
FUZZ - the police

~G~

GANJA - the Jamaican word for Marijuana
GEAR - Heroin
GET OFF - feel a drug's effects
GET ON - use drugs for the first time
GLASS - Crystal Meth
GLUEY - a glue sniffer
GOLD or GOLD SEEL - Marijuana, also called Acapulco
GOODS - drugs
GOOFBALLS - Barbiturates
GRAM - a metric measure of weight
GRASS - Marijuana
GREEN - Marijuana
GUN - equipment for injecting drugs

~H~

H - Heroin

APPENDIX 11 – Drug Terms, p. 4

HAPPY DUST - Cocaine
HARD STUFF - narcotics
HASH - Marijuana
HAWK - LSD
HAY - Marijuana
HEAD - someone who uses drugs frequently
HEAD SHOP - store specialising in the sale of drug paraphernalia
HEARTS - Dexadrine
HEAVEN - Cocaine
HEAVENLY BLUE - morning glory seeds; a hallucinogen
HEAVY BURNER - a person who smokes a lot of dope, a burnout
HEELED - having plenty of money
HERB - Marijuana
HEROIN - china white, fix, horse, smack, whack, mother pearl, H. junk
HIGH - to be intoxicated on drugs
HIP-HOP - refers to a culture that includes rap music, art, dance, fashion, attitude
HIT - a single dose of drugs
HOG - PCP
HOLDING - in possession of drugs
HOME GROWN - locally grown Marijuana; local weed; ditch weed
HOOKED - addicted
HOPPED UP - under the influence of drugs
HORSE - Heroin
HOT - wanted by authorities
HOT SHOT - fatal injection of drugs
HUFFER - glue sniffer
HUFFING - inhaling solvents from a bag

HUSTLE - attempt to obtain drug customers
HYPE - narcotic addict

I

ICE - Crystal Meth
ICE CREAM HABIT - occasional drug use
IN - connected with drug suppliers
ISOMERIZER - used to increase potency of THC in Marijuana

~J~

JAG - extended period of using a drug
JELLIES - Tranquillisers
JIVE - Marijuana
JOINT - a Marijuana cigarette
JOY POPPING - occasional use of drugs
JUICE - Alcohol
JUNK - Heroin, so named because it's never pure when sold on the street
JUNKIE - An drug addict

~K~

KEY - kilogram
KICK - to stop using drugs
KICK BACK - relapse back into drug usage
KIDDIE DOPE - usually prescription drugs
KIF - North African word for Marijuana
KILLER - strong drug
KILLER WEED - strong Marijuana, or marijuana sprinkled with PCP
KILO - 2.2 lbs., also "KEY"
KIT - equipment used to inject drugs

APPENDIX 11 – Drug Terms, p. 5

~L~

L - LSD
LAUGHING GAS - Nitrous Oxide (inhalant)
LEMONADE - poor-quality drugs
LETTUCE - money
LEAPERS - Amphetamines

APPENDIX 11 – Drug Terms, p. 4

LID - one ounce or less of Marijuana
LIGHTENING - LSD
Linctus - Methadone
LINE - a dose of Cocaine arranged in a line on a smooth surface
LIQUID ACID - LSD
LOAD - a large quantity of drugs
LOADED - high on drugs or alcohol
LOCKER ROOM - Butyl Nitrate (inhalant)
LSD - acid, microdots, purple haze, blotters, fry, blaze, tab, dose, gel, pyramid, trips
LUCY - LSD
LUDES - Methaqualone; Quaaludes, Valium

~M~

MAINLINE - inject a drug directly into a vein, to "shoot up"
MAINLINER - a person who injects directly into the vein
MAN - police
MANICURE - remove seeds from marijuana
MARCHING POWDER - Cocaine
MARIJUANA - buds, bhang, dope, goof butt, grass, hash, hay, hemp, herb, jive, pot, rope, stinkweed, stuff, tea, weed, wacky tobaccky, whack,
MARY JANE - Marijuana
MARIJUANA CIGARETTE - bone, doobie, joint, J, reefer, spiff
MATCHBOX - measurement for a small amount of Marijuana
MAZZIES - Tranquillisers
MESCS -Mescaline
MEET - buyer and seller get together
MERCHANDISE - drugs
METH - Methadone or Methamphetamine
METH HEAD - regular user of Methamphetamines
METH MONSTER - person who has a violent reaction to Methamphetamine
METH SPEED BALL - Methamphetamine combined with heroin
METHEDRINE - amphetamine
MICRODOT - a tablet containing LSD
MINT WEED -PCP
MINT LEAF- PCP
MITSUBISHI'S - Ecstasy
MIXTURE - Methadone
MISS EMMA - Morphine
MOGGIES - Benzodiazepines /Tranquillisers
MOLLY – MDMA, or Ecstasy
MONKEY - drug dependency; a kilogram of a narcotic
MULE - a carrier of drugs
MUNCHIES - the hunger that follows after using Marijuana
MUSHROOMS - magic mushrooms, mushroom, shrooms, mushies

APPENDIX 11 – Drug Terms, p. 6

~N~

NAILED - arrested
NARC - narcotic agent
NEEDLE FREAK - a person who prefers to take drugs with a needle
NICKEL BAG - a $5 bag of drugs
NORML - National Organization for the Reform of Marijuana Laws; lobbies for lenient drug laws
NORRIES - Tranquillisers
NUGGET - Marijuana

~O~

OC / OC's – Oxycontin, Oxycodone
O.D. - overdosed on drugs
ON - under the influence of a drug
ON A TRIP - under the influence of drugs
ON ICE - in jail
ON THE NOD - under the influence of narcotics or depressants
OUT OF IT - under the influence of drugs
Oxy's – Oxycontin, Oxycodone
O.Z. - one ounce

~P~

P's - Crystal Meth
PAKALOLO - Hawaiian term for Marijuana
PANAMA GOLD, RED - potent Marijuana grown in Panama
PANIC - drugs not available
PAPER MUSHROOMS - LSD
PAPERS - rolling papers, used to make marijuana or tobacco cigarettes
PARAPHERNALIA - accessories used to take drugs

PCP - (Phencyclidine) angel dust, kools, sherms, high, wet daddies, dust, juice
PEACE PILLS - PCP
PEBBLES - Crack Cocaine
PEPSI HABIT - occasional use of drugs
PERCY - Cocaine
PEANUTS - Barbiturates
PEYOTE - hallucinogenic cactus, buttons
PICKUP - purchase drugs
PIECE - usually one ounce of drugs
PILLS - Ecstasy
PIN - A needle used for injecting
PINKS - Second (Barbiturate)
PLANT - a hiding place for drugs
POPPERS - Amyl Nitrate capsules (inhalant)
POT - Marijuana
POT HEAD - Marijuana user
POWER HITTER - a device (often plastic) used to deliver a blast of Marijuana smoke to the lungs

~Q~

QUACK - doctor

~R~

RAINBOWS - LSD
RAP - to talk with someone; or charged with a crime
RED DEVILS - Seconal (Barbiturate)
REEFER - Marijuana
RIG - the paraphernalia for injecting drugs
RIDING THE WAVE - under the influence of drugs
RIPPED OFF - robbed
ROACH - the stub of a Marijuana cigarette
ROACH CLIP - any tweezers-like device used

APPENDIX 11 – Drug Terms, p. 7

to hold a Marijuana cigarette stub that is too short to hold in the- fingers
ROCKS - Crack Cocaine
ROLEXES - Ecstasy
ROOFIES - Tranquillisers
RUGBY BALLS - Tranquillisers
RUSH - an intense surge of pleasure; Butyl Nitrate inhalant

~S~

SAUCE - alcohol
SCAT - Heroin
SCHOOL BOY - Codeine
SCORE - to locate and purchase a quantity of drugs
SCRIPT WRITER - a Doctor willing to write a prescription for faked symptoms
SENSI -Marijuana
SET UP - to arrange to have a person arrested for drugs; combination of uppers and downers (Barbiturates and Amphetamines).
SHOOTING GALLERY - place where addicts inject drugs
SHOOT UP - to inject intravenously
SHOTGUN - a way of smoking Marijuana, by blowing smoke back through the joint into another's mouth
SINSEMILLA OR SINS - a potent type of Marijuana without seeds grown in Northern California
SKAG - Heroin
SKIN POPPING - to inject a drug under the skin
SKUNK =Marijuana
SLAB - crack
SLAM - to inject a drug

SLANGING - selling drugs
SLEEPER - heroin; depressant
SLEET - crack
SLEIGH RIDE - cocaine
SLICK SUPER SPEED - Methcathinone
SLIME - heroin
SMACK - heroin
SMACK HEAD - Someone who is addicted to Heroin
SMEAR - LSD
SMILIES - LSD
SMOKE - Marijuana
SNAPPERS - Amyl Nitrate capsules (inhalant)
SNORT - to inhale Cocaine through the nostrils
SNOW - Cocaine
SNOW BIRD - dependent on Cocaine
SOLID - Marijuana
SPACE BALL - PCP used with crack
SPACE BASE - crack dipped in PCP; hollowed out cigar
SPACE CADET - habitual user of Marijuana
SPACED OUT - under the influence of drugs
SPACED - unresponsive to surroundings
SPECIAL "K" - Ketamine
SPEED - Amphetamines
SPEED BALL - a mixture of Cocaine and Heroin; "Bombita"
SPEED FREAK - person who repeatedly takes Amphetamines, usually intravenously
SPIKE - needle used to inject drugs
SPOONS - paraphernalia associated with Cocaine, often worn as jewellery
STAR DUST - Cocaine
STARS - LSD

APPENDIX 11 – Drug Terms, p. 8

STASH - a place where drugs are hidden
STEP ON - to dilute drugs
STICK - a Marijuana cigarette STIMULANTS - pep pills
STONED - under the influence of drugs
STONES - Crack Cocaine
STRAIGHT - not using drugs
STRUNG OUT - heavily addicted to drugs
STUFF - drugs
SUGAR CUBES - LSD
SUGAR LUMPS - LSD
SUPERMAN - LSD blotter with Superman imprint
SUPER C - Ketamine
SUPER GRASS - PCP
SUPER ICE - smokable methamphetamine
SUPER JOINT – PCP

~T~

TAB - LSD
TASTE - a small sample of drugs
TEA - Marijuana
THAI STICKS - Marijuana laced with Opium
TINA - Crystal Meth
TOBACCO - butt, chew, weed, cig,
TOKE - inhaling Marijuana or Hashish smoke
TOLLEY - or toluene; a cheap, extremely harmful paint solvent (inhalant)
TOOT - to sniff Cocaine
TOOTER - small, hollow tube (straw-like) to sniff Cocaine
TO PARTY - refers to having a good time using alcohol and other drugs
TRACKS - a row of needle marks on the skin
TRAP - a hiding place for drugs

TRIP - under the influence of drugs
TRIPPER - LSD
TRIPS - LSD
TURF - a location where drugs are sold
TURKEY - a substitute sold as a specific drug
TURNED ON - introduced to drugs, or under the influence of drugs
TWEEZES - a wild variety of psilocybin mushrooms (hallucinogen)

~U~

UNCLE - Federal Agents
UPPERS - Stimulants, Amphetamines

~V~

VALLIES - Tranquillisers
VALIUM - ludes, drunk pills, v's blues

~W~

WACKY TOBACCKY - Marijuana
WASH - Crack Cocaine
WASTED - intoxicated, strung out
WEED - Marijuana
WHITE - Cocaine
WHITE LIGHTENING - LSD
WINDOW - LSD
WIRED - addicted to Amphetamines or Heroin
WORKS - equipment for injecting drugs

~X~

XTC - Ecstasy

APPENDIX 11 – Drug Terms, p. 9

~Y~

YABA - Crystal Meth
YELLOW JACKETS - Nembutal, Barbiturate
YEN - a strong craving

~Z~

ZIGZAG - a brand of rolling papers used to make Marijuana cigarettes
ZOMBIE -PCP; VERY heavy user of drugs

ZOMBIE DRUG – Krokodil (see **Appendix 3**).
ZONKED - extremely high on drugs

Made in the USA
Middletown, DE
23 November 2024

64992748R00060